CW00431256

INTO THE DESERT

INTO THE DESERT

Reflections on the Gulf War

Edited by Jeffrey A. Engel

Contributors

Ryan C. Crocker

Jeffrey A. Engel

Lawrence Freedman

Richard N. Haass

Michael R. Gordon

AND

Shibley Telhami

OXFORD
UNIVERSITY PRESS

OXFORD
UNIVERSITY PRESS

✷ ✷ ✷

SCOWCROFT INSTITUTE
OF INTERNATIONAL AFFAIRS

THE BUSH SCHOOL OF GOVERNMENT AND PUBLIC SERVICE
TEXAS A&M UNIVERSITY

Oxford University Press is a department of the University of Oxford.
It furthers the University's objective of excellence in research, scholarship,
and education by publishing worldwide.

Oxford   New York

Auckland   Cape Town   Dar es Salaam   Hong Kong   Karachi
Kuala Lumpur   Madrid   Melbourne   Mexico City   Nairobi
New Delhi   Shanghai   Taipei   Toronto

With offices in

Argentina   Austria   Brazil   Chile   Czech Republic   France   Greece
Guatemala   Hungary   Italy   Japan   Poland   Portugal   Singapore
South Korea   Switzerland   Thailand   Turkey   Ukraine   Vietnam

Oxford is a registered trademark of Oxford University Press
in the UK and certain other countries.

Published in the United States of America by
Oxford University Press
198 Madison Avenue, New York, NY 10016

© Oxford University Press 2013

All rights reserved. No part of this publication may be reproduced, stored in a
retrieval system, or transmitted, in any form or by any means, without the prior
permission in writing of Oxford University Press, or as expressly permitted by law,
by license, or under terms agreed with the appropriate reproduction rights organization.
Inquiries concerning reproduction outside the scope of the above should be sent to the
Rights Department, Oxford University Press, at the address above.

You must not circulate this work in any other form
and you must impose this same condition on any acquirer.

Library of Congress Cataloging-in-Publication Data
Into the desert :
reflections on the Gulf War / edited by Jeffrey A. Engel.
p. cm.
Includes bibliographical references and index.
ISBN 978-0-19-979628-1 (alk. paper)
1. Persian Gulf War, 1991.   I. Engel, Jeffrey A.
DS79.719.I67 2013
956.7044′2—dc23
2012010283

ISBN 978-0-19-979628-1

Dedicated to the memory of Elkie Rodney,
a caring soul who truly served her public

CONTENTS

FOREWORD

August 1990. I had just returned to Washington from an assignment to Cairo and was awaiting confirmation as Ambassador to Lebanon when the Iraqis invaded Kuwait and was asked to head up the State Department's Iraq-Kuwait task force. For the next several months, I had a front row seat for many of the events described in this book.

The invasion marked the end of the post-World War II Cold War era and the beginning of a new multipolar or nonpolar world in which individual state and nonstate actors found they had much greater latitude to challenge major powers and the old status quo. As I write this from Afghanistan as 2011 draws to a close, I can say with some certainty that this is the world that still challenges us and will for years to come. To study the events of twenty-one years ago is to better understand the present and prepare for the future.

For the United States, this was a defining moment. Would we allow the invasion to stand as many in America argued, or would we roll it back? And if the latter, how and with whom? President Bush answered the first question decisively just days after the invasion: "This will not stand." In so doing, he committed not only to the defense of the Gulf and the liberation of Kuwait but also to American resolve and credibility as the world watched to see how we would respond to the first great challenge after the Cold War.

In the region, where our oil-rich allies had long feared Saddam's Iraq, our decision to fight was greeted with great relief: the United States was a reliable partner and ally. Within days, Saudi Arabia agreed to the hitherto unthinkable—the stationing of American forces on Saudi soil in defense of the Kingdom. From the meeting of Ibn Saud and Franklin Roosevelt in 1944 aboard a US warship in Egypt's Great Bitter Lake, the fundamental understanding between our two nations was a simple one: oil for security. Saudi Arabia would be a reliable supplier of oil to the world market, and America would insure the Kingdom's security from external threat. We lived up to our end of the bargain at a time of crisis, and the Gulf never forgot it. The security arrangements that we subsequently developed with the Gulf States have allowed us to prosecute Operation Enduring Freedom in Afghanistan in 2001 and Operation Iraqi Freedom in 2003. Had we not stood with them in 1990, we would not have had these facilities in 2001 or 2012. New threats have emerged, such as the Iranian nuclear quest. Our regional alliances endure because of our decisions and actions taken two decades ago.

And the Gulf War mattered to the world. In the most sustained and successful diplomatic effort in modern times, the Bush Administration put together a multinational military coalition that included divisions from Egypt and Syria, as well as units from the Gulf. For the first time, Arab states were prepared to confront another Arab militarily under US command. An international coalition that included the Soviet Union in its waning moments provided the legal basis for intervention through a series of Chapter

VII Security Council resolutions. The world understood the economic importance of the Gulf region. But it also understood that unchecked aggression in a nonpolar political environment was an unacceptable threat to international peace and security.

The expulsion of Iraq from Kuwait, of course, did not end the Iraqi threat to the region or its own people, some brief, initial optimism notwithstanding. There has been much debate over whether we should have overthrown the regime in 1991. I personally believe that the decision to stay within the parameters of the Security Council resolutions, which stipulated the withdrawal of Iraq from Kuwait, and our understandings with our allies was not only correct but essential. I was also part of the next episode, traveling in the Kurdish north of Iraq in 2001 and 2002 and deploying to Baghdad immediately after the fall of Saddam in 2003. I returned as ambassador from 2007 to 2009. That intervention and its aftermath also have generated much debate, and that would require another book and another introduction. But now, with the last American soldiers out of Iraq, the nation will chart its own course. Whatever it is, it is unlikely that the new Iraq will ever pursue the aggressive policies of the Saddam regime.

Since the collapse of the Ottoman Empire at the end of World War I, the West and the world has had a huge stake in the broader Middle East. An Anglo-French condominium in the area ended with World War II, and the region became an early theater of engagement between the United States and the Soviet Union as the Cold War took shape. American Presidents from Truman to George W. Bush have promulgated doctrines declaring the region vital to US national security. As we contemplate the consequences of the Arab Spring and continue to fight against terrorists who have attacked us at home and would no doubt do so again if they were given the time and space to organize, it will remain so. Its security and stability will also remain vital to the oil-dependent economies of the West. Our engagement will be essential in defense of our own interests for the indefinite future.

This region has been my life since I began my Foreign Service career as a vice consul in Iran in 1972. I have served as an ambassador six times—in Lebanon, Kuwait, Syria, Pakistan, Iraq, and now Afghanistan. I have seen acts of great courage and vision, and I have seen the consequences of ill-conceived and executed policies. The policies of 1990/91 and their execution were without doubt among the finest moments of American diplomatic and military achievement.

During my tenure as Dean of the Bush School of Government and Public Service at Texas A&M, I had the enormous privilege of coordinating and moderating a retrospective on the 20th anniversary of Operation Desert Storm. Assembled together for the first time since the Bush Administration left office were former President Bush, former Secretary of State James Baker, former Secretary of Defense Dick Cheney, former National Security Advisor Brent Scowcroft and retired general Walter E. Boomer. As they discussed the challenges they confronted, the discussions they had and the decisions they made, one was reminded vividly that people make history, and that people count. In my long Foreign Service career, I have never seen a finer or more cohesive national security team working together when America the region and the world needed them most. This is their story.

Ryan C. Crocker

ACKNOWLEDGMENTS

More than most, this book is a group effort. It originated as the "academic" portion of a day-long commemoration of the 20th anniversary of the commencement of Operation Desert Storm, the active military component of the coalition effort to liberate Kuwait from Iraq. This commemoration occurred in January 2011, ably coordinated by Dean Ryan Crocker of the Bush School before his return to overseas duty. His office masterfully oversaw an event attended by thousands, including Gulf War policymakers. Special thanks to Jean Becker and the Office of George Bush, the Office of the President of Texas A&M, Ambassador Roman Popadiuk and the Bush Foundation, Ambassador Larry Napper and the Scowcroft Institute for International Affairs, and Dean Crocker's able assistants for making the commemoration a memorable success.

The aforementioned academic portion of the day owes its existence to the Scowcroft Institute, and specifically the Ansary Conference Fund ably administered by Ambassador Larry Napper with assistance from Dr. Peggy Holzweiss. Larry did more than anyone to make commemoration of the Gulf War only somewhat less logistically complicated than the original. A highlight of our academic portion of the day were newly released documents from the Bush Library, for which the public and scholarly community have Warren Finch, Robert Holzweiss, and a slew of marvelous archivists to thank. Their work makes the work of writing history possible.

At Oxford University Press, David McBride saw the book to publication, with insightful political, as well as editorial, comments. Thanks as well to Caelyn Cobb for logistical help, and the indefatigable pair of Susan Ferber and Katherine Carté Engel as fonts of advice. Thanks too to Abby Doll and Sarah Saunders, research assistants extraordinaire, as well as Professor Charles Hermann, Dr. Abdul-Reda Assiri of Kuwait University, and Ms. Janeen Wood for their invaluable assistance when the papers that became the chapters in this book were first presented to the public. Mary Finch and Bonnie Burlbaw of the Bush Presidential Library helped locate and secure the pictures included with this book, several published for the first time within these pages. Needless to say, to Ambassador Crocker, Lawrence Freedman, Michael Gordon, Richard Haass, and Shibley Telhami, the thanks of everyone from Aggieland for your insights and thought-provoking commentary and analysis of the Gulf War twenty years on.

Jeffrey A. Engel

CONTRIBUTORS

While serving as Ambassador to Afghanistan, **Ryan C. Crocker** is on leave as Dean, Executive Professor, and Edward and Howard Kruse Endowed Chair at the Bush School of Government and Public Service at Texas A&M University. He retired from the Foreign Service in April 2009 after a career of over thirty-seven years. He served as an Ambassador five times: Iraq (2007–2009), Pakistan (2004–2007), Syria (1998–2001), Kuwait (1994–1997), and Lebanon (1990–1993). He was a member of the faculty at the National War College 2003–2004. From May to August 2003, he was in Baghdad as the first Director of Governance for the Coalition Provisional Authority. He served as Deputy Assistant Secretary of State for Near Eastern Affairs from August 2001 to May 2003. In September 2004, President Bush conferred on him the personal rank of Career Ambassador, the highest in the Foreign Service. Crocker received the Presidential Medal of Freedom, America's highest civilian award, in 2009. In May 2009, Secretary of State Hillary Clinton announced the establishment of the Ryan C. Crocker Award for Outstanding Achievement in Expeditionary Diplomacy.

Jeffrey A. Engel is the founding Director of the Presidential History Project at Southern Methodist University. Until the summer of 2012 he served as the Verlin and Howard Kruse '52 Founders Professor at Texas A&M University and Director of Programming for the Scowcroft Institute of International Affairs. A graduate of Cornell University, he additionally studied at St. Catherine's College, Oxford University, received his Ph.D. in American History from the University of Wisconsin–Madison, and served as an Olin Postdoctoral Fellow in International Security Studies at Yale University. His books include *Cold War at 30,000 Feet: The Anglo-American Fight for Aviation Supremacy* (Harvard University Press, 2007), which received the biannual Paul Birdsall Prize from the American Historical Association for Outstanding work in European Military and Strategic History; *Local Consequences of the Global Cold War* (Stanford University Press, 2008); *The China Diary of George H.W. Bush: The Making of a Global President* (Princeton University Press, 2008); *Rethinking Leadership and "Whole of Government" National Security Reform,* with Joseph R. Cerami (Strategic Studies Institute, 2010); and *The Fall of the Berlin Wall: The Revolutionary Legacy of 1989* (Oxford University Press, 2009).

Sir Lawrence Freedman is the Professor of War Studies and the Vice Principal for Research at King's College London. He holds a Bachelor of Arts degree from the University of Manchester, a Bachelor's of Philosophy degree from the University of York, and a Doctorate of Philosophy from the University of Oxford. Sir Freedman's main research interests are in contemporary defense and foreign policy issues, and he has close links to the Centre of Defence Studies, the Royal College of Defence Studies, and the British Academy. He is the author or editor of twenty-six books, including *A Choice of Enemies: America Confronts the Middle East* (Public Affairs, 2008) and *The Gulf Conflict, 1990–1991* (Princeton University Press, 1995), and has written extensively on nuclear strategy and the Cold War. In 2003, Sir Freedman received the title of Knight Commander of the Most Distinguished Order of St. Michael and St. George.

Michael Gordon, who holds a journalism degree from Columbia University, is the chief military correspondent for the *New York Times*, where he has worked since 1985. Along with General Bernard E. Trainor, Mr. Gordon has written two books including *The General's War: The Inside Story of the Conflict in the Gulf*, which covers the 1991 Gulf War, and the best-selling *Cobra II: The Inside Story of the Invasion and Occupation of Iraq*, which covers the Iraq War that began in 2003. In 2002, Mr. Gordon produced and hosted the award-winning documentary *Deadlock: Russia's Forgotten War* for CNN, which chronicled his risky trip into dangerous and highly restricted areas of Chechnya to capture the scenes of war. Mr. Gordon, together with Steven Engelberg, won a 1989 George Polk Award for international reporting following their series of articles on nuclear proliferation.

Richard N. Haass is president of the Council on Foreign Relations, an independent, nonpartisan membership organization dedicated to helping others better understand the world and the foreign policy choices facing the United States and other countries. Dr. Haass is the author or editor of eleven books on American foreign policy, including *War of Necessity, War of Choice: A Memoir of Two Iraq Wars* (Simon and Schuster, 2009) and has served as the director of policy planning for the Department of State, US coordinator for policy toward the future of Afghanistan, and special assistant to

President George H. W. Bush. Dr. Haass received the Presidential Citizens Medal for his contributions to the development and articulation of US policy during Operations Desert Shield and Desert Storm. Dr. Haass holds a Bachelor of Arts degree from Oberlin College, and the Master and Doctor of Philosophy degrees from the University of Oxford.

Shibley Telhami is the Anwar Sadat Professor for Peace and Development at the University of Maryland, College Park, and a nonresident senior fellow at the Saban Center at the Brookings Institute. He received his Ph.D. in political science from the University of California at Berkeley. Outside of the university environment, Dr. Telhami is a member of the Council on Foreign Relations and has served as a member of the Strategic Environment Working Group in the topic area of Iraq. He also served on the US Advisory Group on Public Diplomacy for the Arab and Muslim World. Dr. Telhami's best-selling book, *The Stakes: America and the Middle East*, was selected by Foreign Affairs as one of the top five books on the Middle East in 2003. Dr. Telhami was awarded the Distinguished International Service Award by the University of Maryland in 2002, and the Excellence in Public Service Award by the University System of Maryland Board of Regents in 2006.

EDITOR'S NOTE

One war. Six perspectives. The purpose of this book is simple: to task scholars, policymakers, and journalists with considering anew a central conflict of the post–Cold War age. Twenty years after the conclusion of the 1990–1991 Gulf War, the passage of time and the addition of ensuing events has surely altered perceptions of the war. Its instigation, meaning, purpose, and aftermath each appear far different with hindsight. There are within these pages perspectives on American foreign policy, American decision making at the crisis moment of 1990, the war as it appeared to international observers and to residents of the Middle East in particular, and the war's long-term effect on American and Iraqi military thinking, which became all too prevalent a topic when conflict arose between the two nations yet again at the onset of the twenty-first century.

There is in fact a quirk of fate within the timing of this book conceived as reflections on a generation-old conflict. It was submitted for publication just as the last American military forces departed Iraq after their post-2003 invasion and subsequent occupation. Rarely have two nations been so intertwined over the course of a generation, with such far-reaching effects, and with arguably as little cultural exchange between the two, as have the United States and Iraq. We hope by shedding light on the first phase of their long struggle to in some small way illuminate the longer story. Contrary to popular wisdom history does not in fact repeat itself. But it does rhyme. By studying our collective history, we can never guarantee selection of ideal choices tomorrow, but at least we can strive for more thoughtful decisions when the time comes.

Jeffrey A. Engel

Princeton, New Jersey

December 14, 2011

INTO THE DESERT

[1]

THE GULF WAR AT THE END
OF THE COLD WAR
AND BEYOND

Jeffrey A. Engel

The Gulf War's full meaning remains elusive, though it is best understood as a coda to the Cold War. Iraq, the Middle East, the United States, and the wider world each retain scars of a conflict ended more than a generation ago. Each remains influenced by the conflict's inconclusive legacy. This book explores those scars, that legacy, and the still evolving meaning of a war hardly gone, hardly forgotten, and increasingly intertwined in a long and complex history of a region then, as now, at the epicenter of contemporary global affairs.[1]

The entire Gulf War was, by standard accounts, a six-month conflict from invasion to liberation. Iraqi troops entered Kuwait on the evening of August 2, 1990. After months of diplomatic posturing and military buildup, they were ejected after merely five weeks of fighting by an American-led coalition. Ground combat required only one hundred hours. Each side, however—or more accurately, every side, given the multitude of players—ultimately claimed victory. Kuwaitis regained their country. Saudis remained free from the horrors and indignity of Iraqi occupation. Israelis survived largely unscathed by Iraqi missiles, while the global economy remained largely free from the type of massive disruption feared absent easy access to the Middle East's precious petroleum. Coalition members found common purpose, shared interests many had not previously recognized, and hope for a more peaceful future.

Rebuffed in conquest, Saddam Hussein's Baathist regime rejoiced in survival. It retained domestic control, emboldened by having endured the world's blunt force. What Iraqi leader Saddam Hussein famously termed the "mother of all battles" turned into a rout for Baghdad's international enemies, though surviving remnants of Hussein's formidable military in time routed his opponents at home. After tenuous weeks in which the regime's days seemed numbered, government forces ultimately repressed uprisings, further solidifying their autarchic sectarian rule. Having suffered Washington's best blows and survived, Hussein became an isolated hero for those equally at odds with American power. His survival alone was proof, he boasted, of his military prowess, political power, and despite the loss of Kuwaiti territory briefly under his control, his ultimate victory in the Gulf War.

Americans in particular perceived the Gulf War as a victory, interpreting their successful ouster of Iraqi forces from Kuwait both as a demonstration of their unrivaled global power at the Cold War's end and salve for painful wounds leftover from recent conflicts. There were no victory parades after American helicopters fled Saigon in 1975, Iran in 1980, or Beirut in 1983. The invasion of tiny Panama in late 1989 paled in comparison to defeat of Iraq's army, on paper among the world's largest and most powerful. Whereas the active phase of Gulf War hostilities was months in the making and thereby anxiety producing, most Americans did not learn of the Panamanian invasion until it was largely concluded. The Central American escapade thus produced a general sense of satisfaction with Washington's regional prowess, but hardly healed lingering wounds from Vietnam and the like. Moreover, fearful of upsetting Eastern Europe's fragile democracies, American leaders had been equally loath to celebrate too loudly after communism's collapse in Europe. "I'm just not an emotional guy," President George H. W. Bush explained of his muted reaction to the fall of the Berlin Wall. Bush refused to publicly bask in the West's Cold War victory, refusing to "dance on the wall" as he repeatedly told advisors and subordinates, and thereby risk potentially undermining pro-Western reformers or spurring a conservative crackdown as the world had brutally witnessed earlier in the year in Tiananmen Square. There had been little cause for celebration in the 1970s and early 1980s; there was too much danger in exuberance at the decade's end.[2]

Americans made up for lost time in 1991. After vanquishing Iraqi troops from Kuwait and successfully defending Saudi Arabia's precious oil fields, Gulf War soldiers returned in triumph. Their parade through New York's steel canyons epitomized the victorious air. Sons and daughters of Vietnam veterans—and more than a few who had served in that war as well—retraced the steps of forebears who had planted similar victory flags in 1865, 1898, 1919, and 1945. Tens of thousands of spectators turned out in celebration, showering their cheers from sidewalks and office windows. Parade organizers special-ordered more than 6,000 tons of actual ticker-tape in a nod toward authenticity for their Gulf War celebration, adding this rare computer-age commodity to untold tons of confetti and shredded phone books. "What other city would show its affection for their heroes by throwing litter at them," their spokesman declared.[3]

It was as much an exhalation as celebration, as though the nation's collective breath, held not just for months of anxiety but through years of lament, was finally sighed in relief. Pessimistic pundits had predicted massive casualties and a protracted conflict against an entrenched enemy willing to deploy the most horrid of weapons. Neither proved true. *New York Times* columnist William Safire caught the air of the day when he wrote, "From the mid-60s to the mid-80s, we slogged through the Slough of Self-Doubt. We lost a war to Vietnam and lost a President to Watergate and lost faith in our know-how when the choppers collided at Desert One. Then the tide turned." Bush was blunter. "The specter of Vietnam has been buried forever in the desert sands of the Arabian Peninsula," he boasted at war's end, no longer wary of celebratory words. The Cold War was no more, he declared, and "the first test of the new world order has been passed."[4]

Victory, and a wholly new world, ultimately proved easier to declare than to secure. Much like the peace of 1919 proved illusory while that of 1945 morphed nearly seamlessly into the nuclear-tinged Cold War, the Gulf War's results proved increasingly inconclusive over time. Kuwait remained sovereign after 1991, and Saudi Arabia (as well as vital petroleum shipping lanes through the Gulf) largely free from Iraqi pressure. Yet Saddam Hussein remained ensconced in Baghdad, a rallying point for anti-American sentiment throughout the Middle East and the wider world, and a thorn in the side to American policymakers unable to secure his ouster at the minimal cost they might budget or politically sanction. Washington appeared globally triumphant to the point of hegemonic after 1991; yet appeared to many critics throughout the 1990s little more than a paper tiger when forced to confront Hussein's persistent rule, and increasingly like an apocryphal elephant frightened by a lowly mouse when presented with speculative evidence of Iraqi nefarious nuclear intent. The United States was newly enmeshed to a greater degree than ever before in the strategically vital Middle East after 1991; yet so too did an overarching settlement between Israelis and Arabs prove beyond Washington's power during either George Bush's Presidency or that of his successor, Bill Clinton. Each strove for, and failed to secure, peace throughout the region.

Bush's "new world order" ultimately proved unruly and dangerous, and in retrospect not immediately superior to the Cold War it succeeded. The post–Cold War era lacked the stability, terrifying at times but at least easily understood, of the long superpower conflict. Fear of such instability had long haunted Bush's advisors, who recognized that the power vacuum created by Soviet decline offered prime opportunity for international mischief and mayhem. "It's tempting to say, 'Wouldn't it be great if the Soviet empire broke up,'" the President admitted privately in September 1989, "but that's not really practical or smart, is it?" The most Washington could do in the face of revolutionary change throughout the communist world, Bush believed, was to "see the situation over there slow down and settle a bit," while keeping reform "moving in the right direction."[5]

The Gulf War's inconclusive end did little to establish an era of calm and stability. Middle Eastern democracy, promised at the eleventh hour by American officials eager to secure domestic and international support for the war, grew slowly in the region's poor soil. Iraq in particular suffered. During the first decade that followed, a litany of indecisive sanctions, diplomatic posturing, civilian suffering, weapons inspections, and no-fly zones pitted Hussein's increasingly isolated regime against Washington and frequently the international community. Hussein, however, remained in power long after George Bush had left the White House. The second decade after the Gulf War's end, neatly punctuated chronologically by the terrorist attacks of September 2001—whose origin can clearly be traced to the aftermath of the Gulf War given fundamentalist fury over maintenance of American troops on Saudi soil following 1991—led almost inexorably to Hussein's further identification as an American adversary by another President named Bush. This far younger President, temperamentally more zealous than his father and far less experienced in global affairs, desired outright regime change in Baghdad and rapid-fire fulfillment of the democratic surge throughout the Middle East the elder Bush quietly envisioned as a long-range goal for the region. The initial results of George W. Bush's war were really never in doubt. In 2003, as in 1991, American forces triumphed on the battlefield. No power on the planet rivaled its prowess in kinetic warfare.

Long-term victory, however, once more proved illusory. After 2003, just as following 1991, American policymakers spent the ensuing years in search of some means to transfer immediate battlefield success into sustainable peace and stability. In the broadest sense, American policymakers after 1991, and again after 2001, searched for an overarching mission absent their Cold War lodestar. They therefore spent a full generation after the Gulf War in search of some path out of the very desert upon which they repeatedly triumphed. The world might have passed its first test of Bush's "new world order" in 1991. Its final grade, however, remains in doubt.[6]

This book examines the Gulf War anew. Its goal is to explain, within the broad categories of history, strategy, politics, military affairs, and public opinion, what that initial war over Kuwait meant to participants at the time; what it continues to mean for journalists, scholars, and policymakers still engaged in the region; and ultimately what the Gulf War might yet come to mean for future generations.

This is thus a book about a conflict, a resonant moment in time, and their still unfolding meaning. This introductory essay places the Gulf War within the stream of international history, arguing that the Gulf War is best understood as a final spasm of Cold War geopolitics and an initial example of the post-Cold War international system whose outlines, and outcome, remains unclear. It is followed by four divergent perspectives on the war. Richard Haass, President of the Council on Foreign Relations and a key National Security Council official during the Gulf War, explains American decision making then and after when confronted with Iraqi threats. Lawrence Freedman, Professor of War Studies at King's College, London, in turn views the war as a global event with far-ranging causes and implications. Michael Gordon, Chief Military Affairs Correspondent of the *New York Times*, explores the Gulf War as a vital moment in war fighting and war planning for Iraqis and Americans alike, while Professor Shibley Telhami, the Anwar Sadat Chair of the University of Maryland, reveals in his chapter the long-term response to the conflict within the Arab world. Collectively, their purpose is to inform readers unfamiliar with these events why they mattered and to remind those whose handle on details has understandably been clouded by so many similar cases, problems, and battles over the same ground and involving the same actors in the years that followed. As William Faulkner once wrote, "the past is never dead. It's not even past." While his words about the American South never rang more true than when applied to the ever-tumultuous relationship between the United States and the Middle East, the past must also be contained and compartmentalized if we are to appreciate its particulars and significance. Because so many of the major fault lines of the Gulf War appear, with a generation's hindsight, to be ongoing if not omnipresent, this book hopes to contain those past themes long enough, at least, to grasp their current meaning.[7]

THE GULF WAR, THE COLD WAR, AND THE STRATEGIC LANDSCAPE AT THE START OF THE 1990S

The Gulf War is best understood as a final chapter to the half-century-long Cold War. By the time Saddam Hussein's Iraqi forces invaded neighboring Kuwait in early August 1990, the long struggle for global dominance between capitalism and communism, championed by the United States and the Soviet Union, respectively, was in Secretary of State George Schultz's famous phase, "all over but the shouting." Washington had won. More accurately, its exhausted adversary surrendered. European communism had failed, having failed to produce the material success or human capital promised in its inception. His economy crumbling and political system stagnant by the mid-1980s, Soviet leader Mikhail Gorbachev initiated an urgent surge of domestic reforms. He simultaneously unleashed pent-up frustrations within Moscow's empire. These Eastern European states, legacy of Soviet triumph at the close of World War II and a principle cause of initial Cold War antagonisms with the West, soon toppled like so many dominoes. Throughout 1989 democratic forces won successive elections in Poland, then Hungary and Czechoslovakia, taking power in a peaceful transition few would have imagined or believed only months before. The Iron Curtain was effectively breached that summer, when Hungary opened its border to Austria; it collapsed in full when the Berlin Wall fell in November, unifying a city, a country, and a continent divided at its very heart since 1945. In 1990 East Germans literally voted their state out of existence. By the close of 1991 even the Soviet Union was no more.[8]

The world had therefore fundamentally changed by the time Iraq invaded Kuwait, and these transformations not only made the

Gulf War possible, they also largely defined its course. Bipolarity and the zero-sum game of superpower competition defined international relations over the previous four decades. The 1990s augured not only a more democratic future and chaotic future, but a more collective one as well. The new global medium of satellite television and the promise of greater connectivity to come produced a sense of optimism and hope rarely witnessed in the twentieth century. People around the world watched, simultaneously, as crowds danced on the Berlin Wall; they would watch, en masse and in unison, as Nelson Mandela walked to freedom in a South Africa nearing eradication of apartheid, and as Chinese students erected their own statue of liberty in the heart of their communist regime's capital. In the words of a chart-topping British rock band, "right here right now, there is no other place that I'd want to be; right here right now, watching the world wake up from history."⁹

The Cold War's end and ensuing Gulf War marked the real coming out party for a global media capable of delivering news of events from throughout the world with heretofore unknown speed. It also marked the start of a singular global media. Not only did policymakers and their publics around the world share information and images almost simultaneously, they turned to a remarkable degree to an increasingly small number of news outlets with resources capable of covering and interpreting global events. More to the point, years before the Internet and blogosphere would democratize reporting and commentary, they turned to the same outlets. Events themselves, and global reaction to them, thus streamlined as never before. When Iraqi missiles rained down on Israel during the Gulf War, to cite but one example, policymakers in the White House, in underground bunkers in Baghdad, in the Kremlin, and in Israel itself all tuned to CNN to gauge their effect. Their respective intelligence agencies no longer broke the news to their political masters. The instead only confirmed or denied what policymakers saw with their own eyes. The ensuing conversations and diplomacy between global leaders therefore began not from unequal starting points of different information and intelligence, as was so often the case in the past, but rather from the new lingua franca of television imagery. Events on the screen were shared; time itself seemed compressed as events impacted countries across the globe with radical speed. Conversely, events not covered by the news media need not have occurred at all for all their minimal impact on international politics.[10]

The democratic surge, whose birth pangs beamed throughout the world, did not always triumph or end bucolically. Regimes rarely cede control without a fight. Neither do revolutionaries typically easily forgive or lightly forget past grievances against their oppressors. Chinese leaders brutally suppressed their own homegrown democratic impulse in June 1989, ironically on the same day Poland's communist regime ceded power in a peaceful election. As US Ambassador to China, James Lilley, explained to his superiors back home, "First of all, this regime wants to stay in power." Beijing's ruling clique deployed a level of violence few governments would endorse, and even fewer could condone. Indeed, in their waning months in power, East German leaders studied the Chinese example for lessons they might put to use in defense of their own regime (against their own people), but failed at the eleventh hour to find heart or stomach for equally repressive measures as crowds of protestors swelled. Amidst much global and domestic criticism President Bush sanctioned the Chinese regime for its excessive violence, having little choice after images of Beijing's brutality appeared on television screens around the world, but left the door open for China's eventual reintegration within the community of nations. A race with profound global import was

thus on: pitting democratic reform aided by an increasingly glob-
alized economy within China, against the regime's ability to buy
off populist desires with sustained economic success. Europe's
communists had already lost this particular race; China's retained
hope. As 1990 began, therefore, the world's most populous country remained an international pariah, though its leaders retained
the trappings of legitimacy, including a crucial seat on the United
Nations Security Council.[11]

Not every totalitarian state weathered the changes of the age, or
gracefully ceded power as in Poland, Hungary, or Czechoslovakia.
Romania's brutal regime ended with sudden bloodshed. Long-
ruling dictator Nicolae Ceauşescu and his wife were captured,
tried, and then gunned down in 1989's final hours. Their televised
fate offered autocrats around the world a visible example of what
awaited their own erosion of power. Soviet leaders in particular
paid heed. Gorbachev knew the cost of failure—in particular if the
result were a conservative backlash and coup—could well be his
own life.

Beyond the personal peril of deposed dictators, Romania
served as a warning for the perils of a collapsing state on other
levels as well. Ethnic groups, in the country's hinterland in particular, violently attacked each other over long-simmering slights
and grievances. Civil war seemed dangerously imminent. Cooler
heads eventually took charge in Bucharest, though the nightmare of ethnic combat eventually occurred in Yugoslavia, offering a dangerous lesson for global policymakers keen to remake
the world: new maps might release ancient animosities. American
policymakers in particular heeded this warning and feared the
specter of ethnic violence in Europe and later in Iraq as well.
So too was change embraced with kid gloves within the Soviet
Union itself, in particular in Lithuania, Ukraine, and throughout

the Baltic States attached to Moscow only during World War II. Local rulers sought separation from decades of Soviet rule, just as the Gulf War reached its peak, only to be initially suppressed by pro-Moscow supporters keen to retain the Soviet Union's physical boundaries even as its government transformed. Where this political tension half-a-world away from the battle lines between Iraqi and coalition forces would lead or end, no one could say, casting a pall over optimistic hopes of post-Cold War superpower solidarity. American commentators widely criticized Soviet rejection of Baltic independence—Washington had never recognized Soviet acquisition of the region in the first place—considering Moscow's determination to retain its Cold War borders at odds with the democratic spirit of the age. Behind closed doors, at least, American policymakers feared the end result of Soviet dissolution. "It's in our interest that the nationalist debate be tempered," National Security Advisor Brent Scowcroft privately counseled Bush. "Perhaps some kind of federation would be better than having all these republics arc off and go their own ways."[12]

Not privy to Oval Office expressions of sympathy for his political plight, Gorbachev found American public critiques of Moscow's policy toward secessionist movements particularly galling. Bush and others seemed willing to overlook thousands of deaths in Tiananmen Square, he lamented, but not his own fitful search for a peaceful resolution with those who desired to tear apart his beloved Soviet Union. He had earlier criticized Bush for deploying American force in support of Filipino leader Corazon Aquino's effort to withstand a coup, and Washington's forceful disposal of Panama's Manuel Noriega, noting on each occasion that American policymakers, though quick to chastise others who employed force for political ends, wholly endorsed the tactic when the force was their own. "You have now given the MFN [Most-favored nation trade status] treatment to China after Tiananmen Square," Gorbachev chastised Senate Majority Leader George Mitchell during the summer of 1990. Therefore, he continued, "what shall we do" to win Washington's favor? "Maybe we should introduce presidential rule...and fire some rounds in the Baltics?"[13]

Neither man realized their conversation was overheard by live television cameras, and subsequently rebroadcast throughout the world. Even savvy reformers required tutoring in the dynamics of the new global media. When Saddam Hussein invaded Kuwait only a few weeks later, such Soviet-American tensions were largely swept aside out of a desire for common resolve in the desert. As we shall see below, however, superpower tensions lurked just below the surface of solidarity.

Gorbachev's frustrations with Washington, and American skepticism over his sincerity in seeking reform or his likelihood of success, reveal a crucial though oft-overlooked dynamic of international affairs at the onset of the 1990s. The Cold War did not have to end well. Superficially that statement could be taken to mean merely that the collapse of the Soviet empire might have unleashed a violent centrifuge through Europe and beyond, driving the continent once more toward its past of war, hatred, and conflict. Such an awful fate was never far from policymakers' minds. Yet suggestion that the Cold War's end need not have ended well can mean something less dramatic though no less profound: the end of bipolarity need not necessarily have made allies out of former adversaries. Washington and Moscow need not have been partners in the journey toward the twenty-first century merely because their twentieth-century conflict elapsed; indeed, Soviet-American tensions in time gave way to Russian-American tensions, owing to powerful conflicting interests revealed, as described below, in the Gulf War's eleventh hour.

The very foundational rules of the international system seemed up for grabs as the 1990s commenced. Isolationists and fiscal conservatives in every continent called for ramped-down international expenditures and commitments. Hawks, meanwhile, cautioned against embracing change, and former enemies, too quickly, lest promises of peace prove illusory and tensions renew. This was not simply a question for Soviet and American leaders. British Prime Minister Margaret Thatcher, for example, who had enthusiastically embraced Gorbachev's promise to end the Cold War back in 1988, fought a rearguard action against alteration of Europe's strategic landscape when German unification appeared on the international agenda. "We do not want a united Germany," she told the Soviet leader a month before the Berlin Wall fell, "because such a development would undermine the stability of the whole international situation and could endanger our security." Change might be embraced by those on the streets, but it caused great trepidation for those charged with maintaining global peace and stability, and in particular for leaders like Bush, Thatcher, Gorbachev, or France's François Mitterrand, all eager to win the future yet uninterested in forgetting the past. "My deepest desire is to keep our radical changes from drowning in blood," Gorbachev told Bush in late January 1991, even as blood prepared to flow in the Gulf conflict. Blood could flow from domestic disorder, from a conflict in the Middle East, or perhaps from a renewal of European tensions of old. In short the world appeared on the brink of change as 1990 began; but it hardly appeared certain that change would lead inexorably to peace.[14]

Cautious and skeptical by nature, the Bush Administration largely hesitated to embrace the Cold War's end, at least during its first year in office. President Ronald Reagan had moved too quickly toward détente, conservatives within the Republican

Party charged, and Bush had made solid cold warrior credentials a central theme of his successful White House bid. Scowcroft, in time Bush's closest foreign policy aide, wasted no time following the latter's inauguration in making clear the new administration's starting position. "I think the Cold War is not over," he declared. Gorbachev "badly needs a period of stability" at home in order to secure his reforms, Scowcroft noted, but "I also think he's interested in making trouble within the Western alliance," hoping to win with a "peace-offensive" what the Kremlin failed to secure through force: separation between Europe and the United States. He noted that Gorbachev's recurrent call for a "common European home" embracing both sides of the Iron Curtain appeared to have no room in its architectural plans for an American wing. Too rapid an embrace of geopolitical change, in other words, might leave Washington less welcome throughout the world, and thus less able to influence events and ensure peace. Others within the administration echoed his skepticism. Deputy National Security Advisor Robert Gates, for whom study of Russia was not only a career but a passion, rarely missed an opportunity to question Gorbachev's promises or their likely success. Similarly, in late March 1989, newly sworn in Secretary of Defense Dick Cheney—with President Bush at his side—warned, "There are those who want to declare the Cold War ended.... But I believe caution is in order." As Cheney bluntly argued, "We must guard against gambling our nation's security on what may be a temporary aberration in the behavior of our foremost adversary." Optimism over the world's awaking from history aside, Cold War era distrust still held sway within Washington's highest policymaking circles, even as the democratic revolution of 1989 unfolded.[15]

Bush refused to concede the Cold War was truly over even as 1989 drew to a close. Caution defined every aspect of his foreign policy, but his hesitation revealed something more profound: he could not declare the Cold War at an end because he could not fully answer the next obvious question of what would take its place. "Is the Cold War the same?" he responded to a reporter's question immediately following his historic meeting with Gorbachev off the coast of Malta in December 1989, a summit initially planned during the summer of 1989 but, following the dramatic fall of the Berlin Wall in November, one that many contemporary observers considered a Soviet concession of Cold War defeat. "I mean, is it raging like before in the times of the Berlin Blockade?" Bush continued. "Absolutely not. Things have moved dramatically. But if I signal to you that there's no Cold War, then its 'what are you doing with troops in Europe?' I mean, come on!"[16]

Bush privately conceded the Cold War's end by the opening months of 1990, but remained at a loss for its replacement. This was not merely a matter of semantics. His administration's ongoing debate over Soviet intentions, Gorbachev's staying power, and the ultimate meaning of their transformative times revealed instead a question of real substance for policymakers whose entire professional experience centered on the Cold War. Bush believed in his nation's global role as protector of international peace and stability, considering this mission the central point of his own military service during World War II and of the decades that followed. He believed as well that Washington's international alliances across the Atlantic and Pacific alike required an identifiable adversary to survive intact. Shared values did not forge nations into allies, he reasoned; shared enemies did. Yet he feared a new wave of triumphant isolationism might curtail necessary American engagement with the world absent some new overriding international mission. "As I look at the world," he admitted in June 1990 with Gorbachev at his side, "the threat is unpredictability and…instability is the threat." He repeated this theme time and again during private conversations with global leaders. He told Germany's Helmut Kohl that same summer, for example, that "the enemy is unpredictability, apathy, and destabilization." He told Britain's Margaret Thatcher, "When I am asked who our enemy is now, I tell them apathy, complacency." Instability terrified Bush and those around him. More fundamentally, he well knew it to be deeply lacking as a rallying cry for his people, or as an underlying glue of international alliances.[17]

This context—a world in flux, leaders hopeful yet cautious about the future, and states reordering their international priorities and very boundaries—is crucial for understanding the Gulf War and global reaction to it. The Gulf War would never have occurred had the Cold War still raged. It would never have been waged, at least as it was, by an international coalition, with United Nations sanction and a superpower at its head, if Cold War tensions still prevailed. Radical transformation of the geopolitical landscape forced regimes large and small, including the United States and Iraq, to rethink their strategic priorities and alignments. The Cold War was all-encompassing and frequently dangerous. But it was also remarkably stable, limiting political shifts save in those few cases (and those mostly on the world system's periphery, such as in Latin America, Africa, or the Pacific Rim) where the superpowers found the stakes worthy enough to compete through proxies but insufficiently important to warrant direct Soviet-American confrontation.

Absent this Cold War lid, relationships, ideologies, and even borders appeared surprisingly malleable. In Washington the word of the day seemed caution. In Moscow, Gorbachev raced reforms against the ever-present fear of a conservative backlash. Chinese leaders, meanwhile, having forcefully blunted dramatic political reform, hoped to buy off lingering discontent with economic growth. In European capitals both East and West such global transitions catalyzed a growing yearning for something new, a transnational union designed to root out the nationalistic causes of conflict and war from centuries past. As the European Council declared in December 1989, "We seek the strengthening of the state of peace in Europe in which the German people will regain its unity.... It also has to be placed in the perspective of European integration." Whether the embryonic European Union would eventually require or even accept either an American or a Russian presence, however, remained an open question.[18]

Trepidation for an uncertain future aside, American and European policymakers and pundits largely interpreted the Cold War's end as a triumph, though not the same. For Europeans the new era validated the ideal of cooperative international relations that had governed the Western half of the continent since 1945: that compromise was superior to conflict, and political union a surefire antidote to historic tensions. The European Union embodied this ideal, and many—Gorbachev, in particular, who had long talked of a "common European home"—hoped to see its embryonic political reach in time extend well across the decaying Iron Curtain.[19]

American strategists preferred a different explanation for the Cold War's demise. The Soviets had not so much given up as been actively defeated, pundits across the political spectrum declared. The global turn toward democracy and markets struck many Americans as validation not only of their power and Cold War leadership, but of their values as well. For some an "end of history," with democracy civilization's final product, seemed at hand. Given the prevailing notion, unproven but no less enthusiastically embraced, that democratic states were less likely to war against each other, an increasingly democratic world augured not only an era of greater freedom, but of peace itself. Bush interpreted the news as confirmation that history itself was on the right course: an American course. "We know what works," he declared in his inaugural address, "Freedom works. We know what's right: Freedom is right. We know how to secure a more just and prosperous life for man on Earth: through free markets, free speech, free elections, and the exercise of free will unhampered by the state." American policymakers largely believed they held the recipe for future international success; they merely needed to put their plan to the test, while keeping their own citizenry interested in the world, and the world interested in America, now that the Soviets were no longer a threat over the horizon.[20]

In sum, the 1990s offered international leaders hope, yet fear as well. Gorbachev wielded an international vision, but lacked the power to implement it on his own. Bush led the world's most powerful state but remained unsure of a future course in 1990. It would take Saddam Hussein to bring them together, as described below, and then in dramatic fashion, to nearly tear their embryonic partnership apart.

1990: THE VIEW FROM IRAQ

Saddam Hussein drew his own lesson from the global transformations ongoing around him, that power remained predominant in defining a state's (or a leader's) failure and success, but the clock was forever ticking on those who failed to act. Powerful nations like the United States had trumped those, like the Soviet Union, incapable of keeping their internal affairs in order and their external threats at bay. So too were both Tiananmen Square and

Eastern Europe ominous warnings that failure to maintain popular support and power at home meant the demise of even the most
authoritarian regimes, especially those—such as Iraq—forged
from multiethnic populaces. Hussein was clearly not one to fear
repression of his own people. Yet even he knew repression had
limits. Retaining power thus required some means of appeasing
his people long-wearied by their nearly decade-long war against
neighbor and rival Iran, a conflict which had seen widespread mis-
ery sufficient to drive down the Iraqi quality of life and life expect-
ancy at a time when the remainder of the Gulf region enjoyed
an oil-fueled economic renaissance. One thing was certain: he
would not be able to look to the Soviets for aid. Iraq had been a
long-standing Soviet client state, but Moscow's days as a financial
provider were clearly over.

From Hussein's perspective, time was short amidst a world
in flux, especially since American strategists seemed intent upon
adding Iraq to the list of toppled regimes. "We have to identify the
sources of danger," Saddam's half-brother and Ambassador to the
United Nations in Geneva wrote in the fall of 1989, "there is no
danger from Western Europe now.... The real danger is from the
superpowers, the United States and the Soviet Union, but at the
same time there are no major problems with the Soviets.... The real
danger is the United States and its follower Israel. The Americans
want to control the region and we are the only obstacle in front of
them." Indeed, Iraqi strategists had long feared their neighbors tilting too far toward the American camp. "What is going on?" Iraqi
Foreign Minister Tariq Aziz asked Kuwaiti rulers in 1988. "Are
you becoming part of the Atlantic alliance?"[21] The implications of
this charge were clear: Arab states that sided too closely with the
West, rather than with their own neighbors, made Baghdad their
enemy. As Hussein lectured his fellow Arab leaders in early 1990,

Moscow's decline afforded Washington opportunity to exert its will. "If the Gulf people, along with all Arabs, are not careful, the Arab Gulf region will be governed by the wishes of the United States." To his mind there was no room among "good" Arabs for "the faint-hearted who would argue that, as a superpower, the United States will be the decisive factor and others have no choice but to submit."[22]

The Bush Administration officially desired closer ties with the Iraqi regime, endorsing limited aid and commercial relations as a means of weaning the Baath Party away from its more repressive tendencies. During the transition period following his election, for example, a Bush advisory team recommended not only continuing the Reagan Administration's strategy of engaging Baghdad in pursuit of improved relations, but speeding the process of peacefully bringing Iraq closer to Washington's orbit. "The US transition comes as we must choose a new direction in our policy towards Iraq. It is up to the new administration to decide whether to treat Iraq as a distasteful dictatorship to be shunned where possible, or to recognize Iraq's present and potential power in the region and accord it relatively high priority. We strongly urge the latter view." Iraq under Hussein was clearly dangerous, if for no other reason than its volatility and key geographic position. Washington's goal was somehow to pacify it without isolating it, to induce Hussein to rejoin at this pivotal moment in history what Bush termed "the family of nations." Iraqis were expected to desire this outcome as well, according to the Central Intelligence Agency's best estimate in 1989. "That estimate essentially said that we believe for the next two or three years," CIA Director Robert Gates later testified, "having just concluded a 10-year [sic] war with Iran, we believe that Saddam will not launch an aggression against any of his neighbors, that he will focus on rebuilding internally, economically and so on." To Washington's way of thinking, Iraqi leaders faced daunting domestic challenges, and any nation desirous of peace and access to global markets in order to rebuild its wounded economy would clearly favor closer ties with the Cold War's wealthy victors.[23]

By the close of 1989 the Bush Administration, just as the Reagan Administration before it, concluded that further carrots, rather than larger sticks, should be used to woo Iraqis toward a more peaceful future with their neighbors and the broader international community. Between 1985 and 1990, the US government approved sale of military equipment and technology to the Iraqi regime totally over $1 billion, while annual trade between the two nations grew from $500 million to $3.5 billion. American policymakers believed Baghdad would in time prove as malleable to trade and commercial ties as the rest of the world, as a dominant lesson they drew from the Cold War's end was that trade brought nations together, in time becoming more democratic and thus ultimately more peaceful as well. "The United States government should propose economic and political incentives for Iraq to moderate its behavior and to increase our influence with Iraq," the National Security Council internally concluded in late 1989, in a policy statement signed by the President as National Security Directive 26 on October 2 under the broad heading, "U.S. Policy toward the Persian Gulf." Numerous high-level official delegations traveled from the American capital to Baghdad throughout the remainder of 1989 and early 1990 to reinforce this point and to bring economic inducements, including teams led by administration officials and Senate Minority Leader Robert Dole, each preaching cooperation, progress, and financial gain.[24]

Iraqis perceived a far different message emanating from Washington. "The tide of history was running against dictators," the Voice of America declared in February 1990, "and had already swept aside several, such as the Ceaucescus in Rumania." That this particular message was broadcast directly into Iraq, with the Iraqi people as its audience, was taken by the government in Baghdad as both an explicit insult, and a direct warning that American policymakers longed to see Hussein's regime join the list of toppled states. Hussein was later called a "cult" leader during an interview by American news correspondent Diane Sawyer. He flinched at this direct insult, but then expressed genuine astonishment at the notion that in the United States, unlike in Iraq, it was perfectly legal to publicly insult the President. Are people who criticize the government not thrown in jail, he asked incredulously? "To the contrary," Sawyer quipped, "they get their own television show." Hussein neither got the joke nor discounted Sawyer's critique, because despite her protestations he believed television reporters spoke the government's mind. This was, after all, the way his country operated. He interpreted her angry interrogation therefore not as aggressive television journalism, of which he had little direct experience, but instead as another threat. "By the end of June [1990] we started to realize that there is [sic] a conspiracy against Iraq," Iraqi Foreign Minister Tariq Aziz explained in a 1996 interview, "a deliberate conspiracy against Iraq, by Kuwait, devised by the United States. So when we came to that conclusion, then we started thinking of how to react against the future aggressors on Iraq."[25]

Saddam Hussein thus entered the 1990s thinking the world was in flux and thus ripe with opportunity for leaders—such as himself—willing to take aggressive steps in the midst of change and crisis. He also perceived himself within Washington's crosshairs, though this was hardly to his mind an unusual position. The Iran-Contra affair of the mid-1980s nearly scuttled Ronald Reagan's Presidency. Oft-forgotten, at least in American circles, amidst the cacophony of allegations stemming from those controversial arms sales to Tehran was that Iraqis bore the brunt of these weapons. American-made antitank missiles aided Iran's conquest of the Fao Peninsula, wrested from Iraq's army in 1986, while American antiaircraft missiles enabled Iran's defense of vital oil terminals in the Gulf. "The Americans," Saddam had privately told his advisors in 1985, even before Iran-Contra when American envoys offered military aid and intelligence for their fight with Iran, "are still conspiring bastards." Public revelation of the arms sales to Iran only enhanced his loathing for American policymaking and exacerbated his belief that Washington desired his downfall. Told to trust the Americans, and to trade with them in order to become more like them, Hussein now found American pledges of peace undercut by their arming of his greatest adversary. "Why are we being punished?" Hussein lamented in 1986. Why did Iraq suffer what he termed this American "injury, this stab in the back?"[26]

Unable to turn to Moscow for help in rebuilding his war-ravaged economy as the 1990s commenced, and wary of American promises given recent history, Hussein looked closer to home for a solution. He looked abroad to the region, and then for more immediate gain, to his own border. The power vacuum created by Soviet decline brought Hussein opportunity to shore up his credentials as a pan-Arab leader following conclusion of the Iran-Iraq war. Having (to his mind) spent nearly a decade actively defending the Arab world from its historic Persian enemy, Hussein believed the time ripe for his nation to assume its rightful place as the leading Arab state, capable not only of rallying regional pride for the sake of economic and political independence but also eventually capable of expelling the Zionist threat from their midst once and for all. "Who can carry this role [of unifying the Arab peoples]?" Hussein rhetorically asked his staff. Surely not Egypt, which had made deals with Israel; and surely not the Gulf States, for whom he harbored deep resentment, earlier terming them "the Arabs of decay, the Arabs of shame." To his mind, "no one else but Iraq" could lead the Arab peoples to their rightful destiny. "Iraq can make this [Arab] nation rise and can be its center post of its big abode." However, he continued, "If Iraq falls, then the entire Arab nation will fall. When the central post breaks, the whole tent will collapse."[27]

Hussein initially sought to burnish his Arab credibility by plucking an anti-Israeli chord. This was low-hanging fruit in a region long infuriated by the presence of a Jewish state. He pledged in early April 1990 to burn half of Israel to the ground if war ever erupted between Arabs and Jews. It did not matter if Iraq was directly involved in the conflict, he warned, ominously as it would turn out given his later rhetoric and actions; when an Arab and Jew fought, he argued, every Arab should take up the fight. The charge was widely disseminated, and condemned, in European and American media circles. Hussein refused to step back from his fiery rhetoric, however, telling Senator Dole during their face-to-face meeting later that month that "Iraq had not threatened Israel, but Iraq will retaliate if Israel attacks...even if Baghdad is pulverized, Iraqi field commanders have their orders. What else is Iraq expected to do? Iraq must try to deter." He further complained to Dole's delegation about the "humiliation experienced daily by Iraqis and other Arabs as they read the western media." Casting himself as an anticolonial crusader desiring only Arab dignity, he similarly explained in April 1990 to Yasser Arafat and a visiting Palestinian delegation that it was time for Arabs to unite behind his leadership in defense of their international rights. "I am filled with faith...if [someone] comes in and shuts the door for the Arabic nation's development and the door of hope for

Palestine [then] we have no hope but to fight. I swear to God that we will fight! We will fight!"[28]

Hussein chose to fight in Kuwait, in time wrapping himself within the broad sheath of Arab nationalism, believing conquest his regime's best chance for survival, and that cloak its best hope for success. He also chose to fight Kuwait because he believed the world's attention elsewhere at the Cold War's end. "Mr. President," one of Hussein's key ministers advised on August 7, 1990—after Kuwait's conquest though still a useful explanation of its timing and underlying rationale—"I believe the present circumstances in the world today have given us the opportunity of a lifetime, and this opportunity would not happen again in fifty years." International leaders were preoccupied with the collapsing Cold War, the Iraqis strategized, believing international opinion cared more for the democratic surge in Europe and China than for the sovereignty of small Gulf States. So long as the oil continued to flow, he reasoned—and Hussein fully expected to sell Kuwait's oil, as financial need underlay the invasion in the first place—the Iraqi leader believed the international community would little care under which flag its oil was produced.[29]

Kuwait was an obvious target. It was close and militarily inferior; it contained vast oil wealth just beyond a long-disputed border; it lacked formal military ties with the United States or any other international power of note; and while Hussein increasingly proclaimed himself a unifying symbol of Arab identity, the Kuwaiti regime was, in the words of one historian, "generally unloved," with "more than a few in the Arab world who would be quietly pleased if they got their comeuppance." Hussein also felt justified. Despite having launched his nation's long war against Iran in a fitful desire to topple the presumably weakened regime in Tehran soon after its own revolution, Saddam Hussein had in the intervening years come to believe his armed forces to be the guardians of Arab culture against the age-old expansionistic power to their East. The significant financial support he received from throughout the Arab world for his war only reinforced this view. Kuwait alone offered Baghdad more than $8 billion in wartime assistance, which Hussein deemed compensation for the blood and treasure his own people paid to protect their neighbors from Iranian influence.[30]

Hussein considered these funds merely a down payment. He expected wartime loans would be forgiven once his long war with Iran came to a close in 1988, and desired additional grants, officially for reconstruction but in fact as reward for Iraq's wartime sacrifices, from Kuwait and the other oil-rich Gulf States. Saudi leaders, wary of incurring Hussein's wrath, heeded his request. They wrote off Iraqi debts following the war, and agreed in March 1990 to a nonaggression and military assistance pact with Saddam. Much like the incoming Bush Administration, Saudi leaders hoped to temper Iraq through friendship rather than exclusion, and Hussein actively encouraged other Arab leaders to follow their example.

Kuwait's government refused to meet Hussein's demands, nor to grant generous financial terms similar to the Saudis. Their rejection of Hussein's pleas prompted a string of threats and blusters from Baghdad throughout 1990, each more virulent than the last, and yet each one perceived throughout the Arab world as merely another negotiating tactic designed to ratchet up pressure on the Kuwaiti regime to pay. At the least, Hussein argued, Kuwait should side with Iraq in approving an increase in oil production limits through the Organization of Petroleum Exporting Countries (OPEC), so that Baghdad could begin recouping its finances on the open market. Comfortable with their secure petroleum profits, however, the Kuwaitis (and others) refused to pump more oil, or to embrace further Iraqi production, lest supply begin to out-pace global demand. Hussein perceived their reluctance more in political than economic terms, however, publicly charging in July that "war is fought with soldiers and much harm is done by explosions, killing and coup attempts—but it is also done by eco-nomic means. Therefore, we would ask our brothers who do not mean to wage war on Iraq: this is in fact a kind of war against Iraq." To buttress his bluster, Hussein quickly moved elements of his Republican Guards, among his best-trained and most-disciplined troops, toward the Kuwaiti border. If the wealthy Kuwaitis were going to wage economic warfare against impoverished Iraqis, he said, his far larger military would have the last say. As he explained to American Ambassador April Glaspie during a private meeting on July 25, 1990, "Victory in the war against Iran made an historic difference to the Arab world and the west," having earlier deplored that "Saddam defends them [Arabs] for ten years [and] they con-sider his defense as a liability. The time has come for every per-son to say…I'm Arabian…I'm Saddam Hussein…Iraq will pay this amount of money to develop the Arab nation and to defend it, [thus] the other Arab countries must pay this amount of money…if they don't we will fight them."[31]

Baghdad had clearly paid much in its war with Iran, suffering more than 1.5 million casualties, and wartime costs in excess of $500 billion. The country began the war with $35 billion in known foreign exchange reserves. It ended the conflict more than $80 bil-lion in debt to foreign hands. Western observers put Iraq's recon-struction needs at $230 billion, if not more. This is for a country with an annual gross domestic product, in 1988, of only $38 billion. "How can we make them [Kuwait] understand how deeply we are suffering?" Hussein asked Glaspie during their soon-to-be-famous July meeting. "The financial situation is such that the pension for widows and orphans will have to be cut." This declaration cued the Iraqi translator and note-taker in the room to break down in tears, simultaneously, for additional dramatic effect. Iraq indeed required financial support to recover from its wartime exertions, Hussein continued once his aides regained their composure. As outside observers such as Glaspie well knew, he could not even easily demobilize his massive wartime army now that peace with Iran had been achieved, as there were quite literally no jobs at home for former soldiers. Given the fate of other authoritarian leaders in 1989 who failed to control domestic unrest, he felt pressured indeed.[32]

Glaspie listened intently to Hussein's long monologue designed to justify his belligerent threats against Kuwait. Hanging in the air were his public warnings that if Kuwaitis failed of their own accord to repay their moral debts to Iraq, by forgiving Iraq's real-world debts and supplying even more in aid, Iraqi troops would take by force what should have been offered in friendship. Though lacking specific instructions, the American ambassador responded in accord with her training. She sympathized with Iraq's plight and the suffering of its people, pledged Washington's continued desire to improve Iraqi-American relations while securing the region's general peace and prosperity, and added that now, as was always the case, the United States would not weigh in on specific border disputes between neighbors. "She had served in Kuwait 20 years before; then, as now, we took no position on these Arab affairs." This was a boilerplate response, employed whenever American diplomats confronted similar historic grievances, useful lest the White House find itself picking sides in countless number of disputed lines on maps.[33]

Glaspie did not believe Hussein would actually invade, and neither did her colleagues back in Washington. American analysts, including those at the Pentagon and the Central Intelligence Agency tasked with monitoring and interpreting Iraqi troop movements, considered Hussein unlikely to attack. Scowcroft's close aides advised as late as July 27, "He (and his people) are extremely bitter toward Kuwait, primarily because economically he is on the ropes. Analysts believe that a shallow incursion into the northern oil field, Rumaylah, cannot be ruled out, while drastic military action is also possible if less likely." Indeed, following her impromptu private meeting with Hussein on July 25, the State Department instructed Ambassador Glaspie to reemphasize the primary thrust of her message to Saddam: that the United States took no formal position on interstate border disputes. More fundamentally, the State Department also instructed Glaspie to restate yet another message she had already delivered on her own, that "we believe that differences are best resolved by peaceful means and not by threats involving military force or conflict." Washington's only concern was that force not be deployed to settle the matter. Indeed, this was the same message, using the same words, that the State Department instructed both its embassy in Baghdad, as well as other American posts throughout the region more than a week before the Iraqi attack: "While we take no position on the border delineation issue raised by Iraq with respect to Kuwait, or on other bilateral disputes, Iraqi statements suggest an intention to resolve outstanding disagreements by the use of force, an approach which is contrary to UN-Charter principles."[34]

Glaspie has not fared well in history. She was accused, following the invasion and in particular following Baghdad's publication of a transcript of her conversation with Hussein, of providing Iraq with a green light to attack, or at least a wink of endorsement, interpreting her statement that Washington "took no position" on the border dispute as tacit approval of Iraqi military adventurism.

Such critiques fail to appreciate the standard and technically accurate nature of Glaspie's reply, one echoed before and after by the State Department. Indeed, talking points prepared by Scowcroft's staff for President Bush, intended for use in a presidential phone conversation with Hussein planned (though for obvious reason, scuttled) for the very day of Iraq's invasion, echo this sentiment. "I again want to underscore my strong belief that it is important to find a peaceful solution to this dispute," Bush would have said, if given the chance. "As we have said before, we do not intend to take sides on the issues currently in dispute between you and Kuwait." Criticism of Glaspie therefore naively fails to appreciate the professional nature of her performance, and at the least that were criticism valid, it should reside far higher up the bureaucratic chain.[35]

In truth very few international observers believed Hussein might attack. He had a long history of bluster, leaving analysts throughout the Middle East and beyond to discount his rhetoric and provocative troop movements, considering them merely negotiating tactics. Similar actions had prompted previous Kuwaiti payments to keep the peace, and most learned observers throughout the Arab World believed this crisis of July 1990 would pass, in the words and judgment of the Kuwaiti Emir, "like a summer cloud," which fairer winds would soon blow away. Indeed having experienced Hussein's extortionist claims before, Kuwaiti representatives had earlier tried to push negotiations with the Iraqis to a head by demanding immediate repayment of all outstanding loans. The broad swath of international leaders, including those intimately familiar with Gulf politics, largely believed this crisis would fade. I "talked to the Kuwaitis, particularly the oil minister, because they were engaged in negotiations with Iraq at the time," the American Ambassador to the United Nations later recalled, "and I asked if they thought there was any possibility the Iraqis would resort to use of force. They said no, absolutely not, that everything is ok, that the Iraqis just wanted to get more money because they owe everybody all this money from the Iran war and we're [Kuwait] going to help them but not as much as they want. That is what the negotiation is all about."[36]

Those who knew Hussein best shared the belief that his bluster was mere bluff. Arab leaders in particular, especially Egypt's Hosni Mubarak and Jordan's King Hussein, repeatedly cautioned Bush against overreacting to what they considered a local matter. This was merely the way Middle Eastern politics worked, they argued. "They [Iraqis] are a bit angry about the situation," King Hussein privately told Bush on July 31, "but I believe that hopefully something will be worked out to the benefit of greater cooperation and development in the area." Bush responded, "Without any fighting?" to which Hussein assured him, "Oh yes, sir, that will be the case." Hussein had even interrupted his ill-fated meeting with Glaspie to receive a call from Mubarak, assuring the Egyptian leader that peace would prevail. Mubarak and King Hussein each continued to stress the need for a peaceful international response even after Iraqi forces invaded on August 1. "I'm worried about the danger to the lives of Americans," a harried Bush told Jordan's Hussein from Air Force One. "Most important, acceptance of this invasion is bad for other countries in the area." Hussein responded by asking Bush, "I really implore you, sir, to keep calm. We want to deal with this in an Arab context, to find a way that gives us a better foundation for the future." Mubarak, who happened to be in the room with King Hussein during this call—the two Arab leaders having come together in a thwarted effort to reduce simmering tensions in the region—concurred that American intervention would only complicate matters. "We are trying hard to solve this" on our own, Mubarak said. "To find a good solution for withdrawal and not throwing away the regime." Bush gave Mubarak the green light to keep trying for an Arab solution. As we shall soon see below, Bush's own national security team already had more active plans in place. "I think if anyone can do it," the President told the Egyptian, "you can be successful." Mubarak's response reaffirmed that such diplomacy was merely status quo in the tumultuous Middle East. "I'm used to these disasters in our area," he said.[37]

A GLOBAL RESPONSE

What passed for politics to Arab leaders struck others as far more dangerous. "They talk about Arab unity," Bush confided to Turkey's President Turgut Özal, "but it's not clear what they mean." Iraq's invasion, and the broader response throughout the Middle East, particularly violated American conceptions of how modern states behaved and responsible leaders treated one another. They interpreted his invasion less as an example of tribal or desert politics than as a dangerous example of a lesson drawn from Europe's past, invoking aggressive leaders from history such as Adolf Hitler for whom force, the standard narrative explained, could be only repelled by force. American policymakers, who by and large rejoiced at the Cold War's seemingly triumphant end, therefore, in time, viewed Hussein's invasion of Kuwait as more than a simple border squabble. It quickly transformed in their minds into a test case for how the international system would operate absent the imposed stability of superpower tension, or whether absent the Cold War the curse of history and of aggressive tyrants might yet return. Deputy Secretary of State Lawrence Eagleburger (who acted in Baker's stead while the Secretary was traveling within the Soviet Union) believed—along with in time the majority of Bush's closest advisers—that Soviet decline verily invited Hussein's aggression. More fundamentally they believed that Hussein's invasion, if not swiftly and properly rebuffed, promised even more of the same. "The Soviets have come down hard," Eagleburger told Bush and the quickly assembled National Security Council the day after the Iraqi invasion. "Saddam Hussein now has greater flexibility because the Soviets are tangled up in domestic issues. If he succeeds, others may try the same thing. It would be a bad lesson."[38]

Eagleburger's argument in favor of a vigorous response to Hussein's invasion in time carried the day, but this is not how the bulk of American leaders reflexively viewed Iraq's aggression. Neither did they immediately leap to Kuwait's defense. On the contrary, the first post-invasion NSC meeting focused almost exclusively on broader—one might argue, more traditional—strategic issues, chief among them the potential impact of Hussein's move on international oil supplies and the transport of petroleum through and from the Gulf. "The meeting itself was unfocused and a sharp disappointment," Richard Haass, then Director of Near East and South Asian Affairs for the National Security Council and a contributor to this book, has argued. "What worried me (and, as I soon learned, Brent [Scowcroft] and the president as well) was the apparent readiness of some in the room to acquiesce in what had taken place. They seemed to suggest there was nothing we could do about it and that instead the focus of U.S. policy ought to be on making sure Saddam did not go any farther and do to Saudi Arabia what he'd done to Kuwait."[39]

This point, and Haass's recollection, should not be lightly overlooked. American policymakers in their first formal discussion of the sudden crisis were largely willing to sacrifice Kuwait for the greater need of global oil supplies. As Hussein predicted, they reflexively cared more for stable oil exports than for sovereignty.

Defense Secretary Dick Cheney, who ultimately argued for a forceful response to Iraq's aggression, bluntly told Bush and his NSC that "the rest of the world badly needs oil" and "have little interest in poor Kuwait." As described above, Bush himself made a similar point to Egypt's Mubarak in their first phone conversation following Iraq's invasion, calling the "most important" aspect of the crisis not Kuwait's fate, but that "this invasion is bad for other countries in the area." Scowcroft later wrote of being "frankly appalled at the undertone of the [NSC] discussion, which suggested resignation to the invasion and even adaption to a fait accompli." It seemed to many in the room, veterans of Tiananmen Square, the Fall of the Wall and collapse of European communism, the American invasion of Panama and German reunification, merely "the crisis du jour."[40]

American policymakers at the time of the invasion focused primarily on the region's true import: its oil. As Ambassador to the United Nations Thomas Pickering, participant in the aforementioned NSC meeting, explained in an oral history released to the public only in late 2011, "The principal, indeed almost the exclusive preoccupation at that time was how do we prevent the Iraqis from invading Saudi Arabia. I said near the end of the meeting, 'I think you've got another problem, that is, what are we going to do about Kuwait? The credibility of your foreign policy rests on your commitments to countries where we have close relationships and not seeing them overrun by somebody else. I think it's a very important question. You're going to have to reinforce Saudi Arabia anyway, but you should begin to think about that.'" As Pickering continued, "If anyone else commented" after he mentioned Kuwait, "I didn't pick it up."[41]

By viewing any action in the Gulf primarily through an oil-tinged lens, American policymakers were merely playing to form. Crises typically produce reflexive responses. The Bush

Administration had already echoed its predecessors in gauging the Middle East's real worth in terms of its most vital export. Oil was the region's only significant global export at the time. In October 1989, even before the fall of the Berlin Wall and all that ensued, President Bush had signed National Security Directive 26, which as noted above called for increased trade and interaction with the Iraqi regime in order to secure closer ties. This National Security Directive also laid bare Washington's true stakes in the region. "Access to Persian Gulf oil and the security of key friendly states in the area are vital to US national security," it read. Moreover, "The United States remains committed to defend its vital interests in the region, if necessary and appropriate through the use of U.S. military force, against the Soviet Union or any other regional power with interests inimical to our own."[42]

The formal language of this document should not obscure its central point: that what mattered to Washington most of all about the region was not the safety and stability of its governments per se nor the well-being of their peoples—such humanitarian arguments would, ironically, be given greater weight by the aftermath of the Gulf War, as briefly noted below—but rather their continued export of oil. American policymakers might have let Arab cultural norms of inter-state behavior run their course in a region less vital; neither would have they cared so much for the first "test case" of the post-Cold War international system if aggression had occurred in a region devoid of vital stakes for the entire global community. Washington cared about Kuwait, and vulnerable Saudi Arabia just beyond, because oil made the world run, and because the post-Cold War world—including all its hopeful promises of democratic peace and a new age without dictators—would grind to a halt in its absence.

This was long-standing American policy. In 1943 President Franklin Roosevelt visited Saudi Arabia in order to shore up relations well before the country's oil concessions were fully developed. Over the ensuing decades his countrymen brought not only engineering know-how but also a brand of proselytizing Christianity that often put the two governments at odds. Saudi officials were given remarkable leeway by their American counterparts, because their exports were so valuable. In 1980 President James Carter even threatened nuclear war against any state interested in dominating the Middle East's oil. Carter's immediate target was the Soviet Union, whose invasion of Afghanistan the prior year renewed Cold War tensions, in large part because Moscow appeared bent on spreading its control over the very lifeblood of the international system that increasingly flowed through the Gulf. "The region which is now threatened by Soviet troops in Afghanistan is of great strategic importance: It contains more than two-thirds of the world's exportable oil," Carter said. "Let our position be absolutely clear: An attempt by any outside force to gain control of the Persian Gulf region will be regarded as an assault on the vital interests of the United States of America, and such an assault will be repelled by any means necessary, including military force."[43]

Nothing that occurred between Carter's declaration of 1980 and the Iraqi invasion of 1990 diminished the weight and intent of the Carter Doctrine. It was never rescinded by subsequent administrations. On the contrary, both Presidents Ronald Reagan and George Bush publicly emphasized that Washington's principal strategic goal in the Gulf was the free flow of oil. By the mid-1980s American naval vessels escorted Kuwaiti vessels through perilous Gulf waters, though at the time Iran and not Iraq appeared the primary threat. Cold War calculations drove American policymakers during this crisis, because as Reagan candidly explained in 1987, even in the era of *Glasnost* and *Perestroika*, the region's oil supplies were so valuable that "if we don't do it [safeguard Gulf shipping] the Soviets will."[44]

Bush's national security team restated the region's principal importance, defined almost exclusively in terms of its oil, on the very eve of the Iraqi invasion in 1990. Noting Baghdad's bluster toward Kuwait, Defense Secretary Cheney charged his principal strategist, Undersecretary of Defense for Policy Paul Wolfowitz, with reassessing Washington's strategic priorities in the region. On July 26, or less than a week before Iraq's invasion, Cheney thought enough of his deputy's response to pass his memorandum, along with endorsement of its ideas, to Baker and Scowcroft and their staffs. Wolfowitz's conclusions were clear: "the fundamental US interest in the security of the Persian gulf is oil. The United States and other industrial countries will be increasingly dependent on oil from the region to meet their energy needs in the next decade." As Wolfowitz further explained, global reliance on Gulf oil was "an inevitable trend," and not only the American but more broadly the global economy would shutter to a halt absent this vital energy source. It would therefore, he concluded, "be inimical to US interests to permit any power—including Iraq—to gain dominance over Gulf oil supplies. Such dominance by a single country would enable it to dictate oil prices and production, placing the economies of the US and its allies in an extremely vulnerable position that would become more precarious as Western dependence on Gulf oil continued to grow."[45]

As a coda to his argument Wolfowitz conceded that "beyond our specific interest in oil," other factors influenced American thinking toward the region, including Washington's historic interest in maintaining global principles of unhindered transit and support for Israel. "Finally," he concluded, "against the background of US drawdown in Europe, US actions will be carefully watched for signs of a more general US inclination to disengage." These final rationales for American strategic concern in the Gulf—the principle of freedom of the seas, Israel's future, and lastly visible demonstration of continued American engagement in global affairs after the Cold War—were but addendums to his thinking. For Wolfowitz, and by extension as noted above for Cheney and for the majority of American top policymakers, the initial and ultimately the fundamental interpretation of Hussein's assault on Kuwait was not as an assault on civility or a new world order, even though these would become the public rationales for their war, but rather as primarily an attack on global petroleum interests. Privately, with no one but history watching, the Bush Administration wasted little time in boring in on the truth: Kuwait's sovereignty mattered far less to the world than its oil.[46]

In sum, what Bush's national security team in Washington reflexively cared about most in August 1990 was what American policymakers wanted throughout the Cold War as well: unhindered Gulf exports at minimum cost. It is small wonder, therefore, that Bush overruled his Arab colleagues with their advice to keep the matter a local affair, and the hesitancy of his own national security establishment still feeling the long-term hangover of defeat in Vietnam and expulsion from Lebanon, by forcefully declaring on August 5, four days after Hussein's attack, that Washington would work to reverse Iraq's occupation of Kuwait. "Are you disappointed in the failure of the Arab nations" to secure a peaceful resolution to the crisis, one reporter asked. "Well, I was told by one leader that I respect enormously—I believe this was back on Friday—that they needed 48 hours to find what was called an Arab solution," Bush replied. "That obviously has failed. And of course, I'm disappointed that the matter hasn't been resolved before now. It's a very serious matter." Then came the statement thereafter linked to his overall response to the sudden crisis, words that revealed not only

Bush's intent, but after months of strategic wandering absent his Cold War lodestar, his newfound purpose as well: "I view it very seriously, not just that but any threat to any other countries, as well as I view very seriously our determination to reverse out this aggression.... This will not stand. This will not stand, this aggression against Kuwait." "I've got to go," Bush continued. "I have to go to work. I've got to go to work."[47]

THE GULF WAR ITSELF, AS UNEXPECTED PRELUDE TO THE NEW WORLD ORDER

American policymakers in time interpreted, and more importantly explained, their response to Iraq's invasion of Kuwait in both global and historic terms, far beyond the region's importance as an energy producer. For them, Iraq's invasion revealed the fearful potential of a Hobbesian world of conflict and anarchy absent Cold War stability. Since World War II's end, every strategic move by one superpower had prompted an equal response from the other. In hotspots around the world, from Berlin to Korea to Cuba and back to Asia again, every potential gain for one was countered by the other in a strategic chess match considered by both sides a zero-sum game of global power and prestige.

Not so when Saddam Hussein invaded Kuwait. For the first time since 1945, Washington and Moscow appeared to be on the same page, at least initially. At no previous time since World War II, and certainly not after Carter's 1980 threat, could one superpower have moved an entire army into one of the world's most sensitive regions without prompting a tense if not violent reaction from its main global competitor. Yet not only did the United States lead just such an international coalition into the very heart of the globe's greatest energy supplying region, in order to strike one of the Soviet Union's principal client states, but Soviet leaders actively aided this American-led thrust. In 1946 Soviet forces attempted to gain the upper hand in oil-rich Iran; in 1973 they threatened to use the Israeli-Arab conflict as an opportunity to inject force into the region; and in 1979 they drove into Afghanistan in hope of securing clearer access to the Gulf's unparalleled energy supplies. In each case, the Cold War erupted anew. Indeed, historians often characterize the Cold War itself as not one single contest but instead several, with moments of particular international tension interspersed by periods of relative détente. It is no coincidence that the two greatest periods of escalating tensions, the late 1940s and the early 1980s, arrived immediately after Washington and Moscow nearly came to blows over the Middle East's vital oil. For policymakers of the early 1990s, therefore, unaware of the future that lay ahead but wary of reliving the past, the Gulf War threatened to scuttle all that the Cold War's end promised.

Instead, the Gulf War, at least initially, reaffirmed for leaders in both superpowers their era's potential. Bush termed the Cold War's end the "one new ingredient" that truly separated the Gulf War from all that came before. "We can now work with the Soviets to help resolve the issue," he privately told Turkey's leadership the day after Hussein's invasion. Secretary of State James Baker, for one, did not fully believe the Cold War over until he stood shoulder-to-shoulder with his Soviet counterpart in criticizing the Iraqi invasion of Kuwait. Purely by coincidence, Baker and Soviet Foreign Minister Eduard Shevardnadze were together when news of the Iraqi invasion first broke. They were thus able to devise a common rhetorical response before Baker's quick return back to Washington. Long-time State Department hand Dennis Ross, Baker's main aide for the trip, recalled telling Shevardnadze and his deputy that "You know, in our little meetings of the four of us, Baker and me and the two of you, we've talked a lot about the potential for partnership. We've talked a lot about the idea that we're not only no longer going to be adversaries, but that we don't have to limit what we do to cooperating. We can actually think about areas where we set a tone, we set a direction and we become partners. This is one of those events that we need to respond in a similar way. We have to be on the same page."[48]

The Soviets quickly agreed, leading to a level of superpower cooperation unimaginable only years before. Moscow did not send troops, but neither did the Kremlin utilize its veto in the United Nations' Security Council to thwart Washington's organization of a forceful response. As Gorbachev explained in September 1990, when standing before reporters with Bush at his side,

> Our two great states are undergoing a trial. This is a test of the durability of the new approach to resolving world problems. And as we enter upon a new peaceful period and as we emerge from the cold war, we see that no less efforts are necessary in order to find ways and means in this period of peace to meet the new situation and to tackle all problems that may arise.... And the fact that today we have taken a common approach to such difficult problems—problems which may well have tragic consequences for the whole world, not just for the peoples of that region—demonstrates that we still are moving forward in the right direction and that we are capable of resolving the most difficult and the most acute problems and to find appropriate responses to the challenges of our time.

For Baker, as for many international leaders, such Soviet-American accord was not only without easy precedent, it was also breathtaking. "The entire planet is in this madman's [Saddam Hussein's] debt," Baker later explained. "His brutal invasion of Kuwait provided the unexpected opportunity to write an end to fifty years of Cold War conflict with resounding finality."[49]

The Gulf War helped frame Bush's post-Cold War worldview. It confirmed his hope that a new era of international relations had truly arrived, alleviating in particular his fear that global instability coupled with Cold War triumphalism would foster American lethargy. With Soviet and American leaders on the same side, the crisis that erupted when Iraqi forces invaded Kuwait instead offered an immediate opportunity for the international system to function, with multilateral force and near unanimous consent, just as the founders of the United Nations had first envisioned in 1945, well before Cold War tensions scuttled their more optimistic plans. That the crisis erupted between recognized members of the United Nations—and not between disparate ethnic groups or secessionist elements of a recognized state—fit well with Bush's conception of international politics, in which states played the primary role, and recognized leaders of recognized states held the moral and political responsibility for ensuring stability above all else. This was just as the United Nations founders envisioned, to Bush's way of thinking, and with the Cold War finally gone, that body and the entire international system could finally function as promised—a promise that had motivated Bush's own military service nearly a half-century before. "Nothing of this importance," Bush explained of the Gulf War in 1991, had occurred in the world "since World War II." Considering all that had occurred in the international system since 1945, including the dramatic collapse of European communism in 1989, this was quite an audacious statement indeed. Yet it was also a planned statement, offered not off the cuff but instead before Congress and the watching world, and thus indicative of Bush's considered thoughts. The Gulf War mattered, to Bush, because it offered opportunity to reset the international community's clock back to when international relations seemed pure: back to 1945, back to his youth in fact, when tyranny was defeated and long-term peace seemed at hand, but before the Cold War ruined that idyllic future.[50]

Gorbachev agreed with Bush's interpretation that the Gulf War offered a unique opportunity to demonstrate superpower solidarity, at least, initially. Eager to show Washington and the Western world that his promises of Soviet change were real and lasting, he cast his lot with his former enemies despite apprehension within his own government. As noted above, when he and Bush met in September 1990, Gorbachev went to great pains to present a common front in opposition of Iraq's aggression. Equally, if not more important, he stressed this point behind closed doors as well. "I think this crisis is a test of the process we are going through in world affairs and of a new US-Soviet Union relationship," he told Bush. "I am thinking if we can't cope with this conflict, a new world order can't come in." As we shall soon see, however, implicit in Gorbachev's promise of cooperation lay an abiding threat: that failure to coordinate with Soviet needs within this brewing crisis might scuttle the very notion of East-West détente.[51]

Bush announced his "new world order" vision two days after his conversation with Gorbachev—though Scowcroft claims he and the President hit upon the term while fishing weeks before, when the failure to haul any catch left sufficient time for the two men to talk in depth. Harkening back to his conception of the post-1945 founder's intent, Bush instead argued for a world system "where the United Nations, freed from Cold War stalemate, is poised to fulfill the historic vision of its founders. A world in which freedom and respect for human rights find a home among all nations." Bush thought that the end of the Cold War offered his generation a "rare opportunity to move toward an historic period of cooperation," one that was "freer from the threat of terror, stronger in the pursuit of justice, and more secure in the quest for peace.... A hundred generations have searched for this elusive path to peace, while a thousand wars raged across the span of human endeavor." It should not be missed that Bush's new world order was not intended to be perfect. Terror would be, he said, not eliminated but diminished. So, too, would justice be more prevalent, though not necessarily universal, and security enhanced if not guaranteed. Ever a realist, the world Bush promised would not be perfect, only better than what had come before. The new world would be, he promised, "a world quite different from the one we've known," even if it would look remarkably familiar to the world American leaders at midcentury had once envisioned.[52]

American diplomats secured an increasingly wide-ranging series of United Nations resolutions in the weeks and months that followed the Iraqi invasion, providing both legal and moral authority for the use of force to eject Iraqi troops from Kuwait. Such multilateral consent, deploying multilateral force—albeit with the implicit understanding of great power military force at its back—was at the root of Bush's conception of how the post-Cold War world would work. Having spent much of 1989 skeptical of change, and the first seven months of 1990 determined to forge something sustainable from the ashes of the Cold War, and having lamented that instability might reign absent a driving international ethos for the United States and for its allies, Bush found a purpose in Hussein's assault. "Our approach was to encourage [Soviet leader Mikhail] Gorbachev and the Soviet Union and to do all we could to facilitate the peaceful unification of Germany," he explained. "Then, of course, when Kuwait was invaded by Iraq, there was a real opportunity to further constructive change by getting the Soviet Union to support us in the U.N., and indeed, in the forthcoming battle to free Kuwait."[53]

In hoping that the new world order might prove an improvement over the threat of Cold War global conflagration, but in downplaying its potential perfection, Bush proved more right than he hoped or realized. By the time the Gulf War ended, so too in many ways had the brief honeymoon period of Soviet-American relations after the Berlin Wall's collapse. By February 1991, as Gorbachev struggled to maintain domestic control in the face of mounting economic and political quandaries, Soviet strategists feared anew the growth of American power in the valuable Gulf region. Moscow's initial optimism over the potential for full East-West reconciliation and collaboration had largely evaporated, sullied by months of difficult negotiations over contentious issues such as German reunification, NATO expansion, and help for the ailing Soviet economy. By year's end their regime would itself be gone. With Gorbachev's ouster departed as well the fragile hope of Russian-American cooperation based on the growing friendship and personal trust between each nation's leaders. The Russian state that emerged would be nominally more democratic, but Russian President Boris Yeltsin never found the personal intimacy with Bush that Gorbachev had enjoyed. Bush learned to trust Gorbachev, but it took time for him to appreciate the cerebral Soviet leader's virtues and true dedication to reform. His administration gave the hard-drinking and hard-living Yeltsin little in the way of trust and was itself voted out of office before the two men had time to develop any real personal chemistry.

The Gulf War nearly disrupted whatever personal trust Gorbachev and Bush had developed by the start of 1991. The two leaders stood side-by-side in condemnation of Iraq's aggression during the fall of 1990. Gorbachev, however, appeared at the eleventh hour to back away from full support of the UN mandate to liberate Kuwait. Months of military buildup, political wrangling within Washington producing a razor-thin congressional mandate for military force, and failed last-minute Iraqi-American negotiations led by January 1991 to expectation that the war would soon start. It began as an air war, with the first coalition sorties striking Iraqi targets on the evening of January 17. As American missiles and bombs rained down on Baghdad—where many Soviet officers and officials had spent time or made friends—the Russians had had enough. Both leaders feared that the promise of a new post-Cold War international order was indeed about to break on the rocks of far older antagonisms. "George, my concern is that we make sure not to lose the opportunity now that we have attained strategic objectives," Gorbachev argued as he appealed to Bush to halt the bombing campaign before the ground phase of the conflict could begin. "We have taught a lesson to the aggressor. Our new US-Soviet cooperation, the spirit of our common values, means it is important to do the right thing," he said. The right thing, Gorbachev argued, was to halt the bombing, without further casualties or embarrassment to the Iraqi regime. Gorbachev was particularly blunt. If Bush wanted to preserve Soviet cooperation for the new world order, he must "stop in this phase."[54]

This plea for leniency, and Moscow's attempts to broker a last-minute peace, reflected Gorbachev's own vision for the post-Cold War world, one that had animated both his initial drive for reforms within his own country, and then his subsequent overtures to the United States and to Europe for an entirely new system of international affairs based less on pure power than on the power of shared values. He told Baker as much in August 1990, when the Gulf Crisis first broke. "For his part," the Secretary of State reported to Bush, "Gorbachev's image of the new international order is such that he has a hard time reconciling the fact that we might need to use force in this initial test...he said as much to me today, observing that we want this era to be different from the cold war and based on different kinds of norms." When it appeared that force would eventually be deployed to expel the Iraqis from Kuwait—with the entire world watching the destruction on television—Gorbachev appealed once more for peace. His own vision of the post-Cold War world did not include deployment of hegemonic force, and surely not vivid demonstration that American force and power widely exceeded his own by 1991.[55]

Bush feared in Gorbachev's words the very real threat that this new world order might die in its crib. It was one thing to fear instability in the post-Cold War world; it was quite another to rekindle Soviet-American tensions. Hussein would not give in, Bush believed, and would surely not be impressed by a limited air campaign. He would interpret any halt of the bombing as demonstration of international weakness, not moral resolve. "To be very candid with you," he told his Soviet counterpart in late February, immediately before the ground war kicked off, "we have no trust anymore in anything the man [Hussein] says." More importantly, Bush pleaded, the world needed to see the real power behind the new world order; it needed to witness the lesson that aggression would not pay, so long as the great powers remained in lockstep on the side of stability. "Let's not let this divide the US and the Soviet Union," Bush pleaded a month later, after coalition ground forces began their long-anticipated assault. "There are things far bigger than this conflagration which is going to be over very soon."[56]

By this point in their discussion, and in their relationship, Gorbachev clearly realized he had overstepped his bounds, noting in particular the growing tension in Bush's voice over his repeated injections of Soviet diplomacy into American war making. Bush was tired, after months of planning and politicking the Gulf War appeared ready to enter its final phase, and his reserves of sleep and patience were dwindling. His voice cracked with frustration, prompting Gorbachev to caution, "George, let's keep cool," he said. "Although, of course, all of us are human beings, I think both of us understand that what we need is not Saddam Hussein—his fate has been determined. Our concern is to take advantage of the opportunity before us in order to obtain the goal we set together within the framework together in the UN Security Council and also prevent a tragic phase in the further development of the conflict." The goal for both men in 1990 and 1991, when responding to the Iraqi invasion of Kuwait, was to reassert their broader vision of the future of the international system. In time, as American power grew—and as American power was on display for the world to see in the quick destruction of Hussein's forces—and as Soviet power continued its long decline, their visions diverged. So too, in time, did their nations.[57]

AFTERMATH AND IMPLICATIONS

The Gulf War was thus a Cold War tale, and yet at once the onset of something new. It began because the Soviet Union disintegrated; was made possible only because Moscow and Washington initially agreed to rebuff Hussein's threat to their perceived new world order; and ultimately in its climax threatened to disrupt the very foundations of peace long-sought by leaders on both sides of the now defunct Iron Curtain. By displaying to Soviet and American leaders the fragility of their post-Cold War cooperation, it also revealed in time the unstable nature of the international system absent their protracted superpower fight.

The Gulf War also marked a new period of American engagement in the Middle East. Before the conflict Washington lacked a single defense pact with any Gulf State save Bahrain. American ships routinely patrolled the vital waters, ensuring free passage of oil-laden ships, but this was an offshore presence in the truest sense of the term. Only a fortnight before the Iraqi invasion one of Secretary Baker's key aides, Margaret Tutweiler, reminded reporters that "we do not have any defense treaties with Kuwait, and there are no special defense or security commitments to Kuwait." Indeed in the days leading up to the Iraqi invasion of August 1990, as threats from Baghdad grew in tone and frequency, only the United Arab Emirates agreed to joint military exercises with American forces as a sign of deterrence. There were at the time of Iraq's invasion no American troops in Saudi Arabia, Kuwait, or within reach of the disputed border. Their absence, and the political baggage their appearance would carry for any Arab state that condoned their presence, bolstered Hussein's calculations of success. As he candidly told Ambassador Glaspie on the eve of conflict, he "felt secure [from attack], secure in the belief that no Arab Government would ever allow us to use their land for that purpose."[58]

Within three months of Iraq's invasion more than 500,000 American servicemen and women found themselves in the desert or nearby. Three hundred lost their lives in the ensuing conflict. In the Gulf War's immediate wake, and for the ensuing two decades, tens of thousands of American soldiers, sailors, airmen, and marines called the Gulf their overseas home. Twenty years later more than 5,000 American military personnel have paid the ultimate sacrifice in service in Iraq. Total financial costs for the first Gulf War, the intervening period, and the second which began in 2003, can only be counted in the trillions, at least three trillion dollars according to the calculations of at least one Nobel Prize winning economist for the second Iraq war alone, with even more projected in future costs once long-term pension and medical costs are included. Iraqi losses, human and financial, are difficult to quantify with reliability, but the death toll clearly reached into the hundreds of thousands over the entire generational-long conflict. Perhaps thirty thousand Iraqis, civilians and soldiers alike, perished in Kuwait's liberation in 1991. Millions more have seen their lives irreparably changed and disrupted since, with particularly horrific frequency since 2003.[59]

Such damaging consequences of a long-term direct American presence in the region, or in Iraq itself, were hardly unimaginable in 1990 and 1991. Significant political opposition swelled in response to Bush's decision to send sufficient force to liberate Kuwait, and in particular after it became apparent that Bush was willing to deploy American force, absent a congressional declaration of war, for that purpose. Despite advice to the contrary from more hawkish segments of his administration, Secretary Cheney in particular whose vision of a strong chief executive accepted few congressional constraints in the field of foreign policy, Bush eventually sought congressional sanction for hostilities, winning Senate approval by the narrowest of margins in early January 1991.

Opposition was not simply partisan, but heartfelt. Lingering memories of previous military debacles, including not only Vietnam but also Beirut and Tehran, mounted and multiplied as war approached. *Time* Magazine featured on its cover an American soldier in full chemical-weapons gear, astride the stark headline: "Are We Ready for This?" Public agitation grew when media reports revealed the Pentagon had shipped upwards of 30,000 body bags to the region in preparation for potential coalition casualties.

Doubts surfaced even within Bush's own Oval Office. "I know you're aware," Secretary of State Baker privately cautioned the President, "of the fact that this has all the ingredients that brought down three of the last five Presidents: a hostage crisis, body bags, and a full-fledged economic recession caused by forty-dollar oil." As Senate Majority Leader George Mitchell argued, the risks of war were great, and greater still if the initial response in defense of Saudi Arabia grew into a long-term political and military commitment to the region. These included, "an unknown number of casualties and deaths, billions of dollars spent, a greatly disrupted oil supply and oil price increases, a war possibly widened to Israel, Turkey, or other allies, the possible long-term American occupation of Iraq, increased instability in the Persian Gulf region, long-lasting Arab enmity against the United States, a possible return to isolationism."[60]

Looking back we can see that few of these things occurred in the immediate wake of the Gulf War; but that arguably all of Mitchell's fears—untold casualties, billions of dollars lost, disrupted markets and disaffected allies leading to a new Arab-American hostility and homegrown isolationism—all returned in time to haunt the United States. They did not occur immediately in 1991, however, largely because Bush refused to exceed his United Nations mandate to liberate Kuwait, and in turn refused to proceed on to Baghdad in order to ensure Hussein's demise. In truth, none within the President's inner circle expected Hussein to long survive. Iraqis themselves would take care of their defeated dictator, Bush reasoned, whether in a popular uprising or an internal coup. He refused to put American lives at risk for a result, Hussein's ouster and demise, he expected in any event. "Whose life would be on my hands as the commander-in-chief," Bush told a gathering of Gulf War veterans in 1999, "because I, unilaterally, went beyond the international law, went beyond the stated mission, and said we're going to show our macho? We're going into Baghdad. We're going to be an occupying power—America in an Arab land—with no allies at our side. It would have been disastrous."[61]

In 1991, as the war reached its violent peak, further invasion and occupation of Iraq seemed not only dangerous, but unwarranted. "For years," Baker later recalled, "the question I was most often asked about Desert Storm is why we did not remove Saddam Hussein from power." There were many reasons, Baker explained, including the difficulties of postwar occupation, the dangers of urban warfare to American troops and Iraqi civilians, the threat of sectarian rifts within Iraq, and the legal difficulties of exceeding the United Nations mandate to liberate Kuwait. "As events have amply demonstrated," Baker sardonically noted in 2006, "these concerns were valid. I am no longer asked why we did not remove Saddam in 1991!"[62]

Baker's quip only reinforces the lingering notion, already prevalent in 1991, that the Gulf War's end was incomplete. Hussein, of course, proved remarkably resilient, to the surprise of most if not all international observers. By the time the aforementioned parade of troops marched through New York in celebration of the desert triumph, several months after the formal cessation of hostilities, 72 percent of Americans polled approved of their nation's use of force to liberate Kuwait. A nearly equivalent 69 percent of Americans polled, however, also believed their nation should have continued the fight until Hussein was removed from power. Since the war's end Bush's overall approval ranking had dropped from an astronomical 90 percent at its wartime peak to a still remarkable 75 percent, a drop that presaged his eventual inability to translate his foreign policy successes into reelection at the polls. Both Ross Perot and Bill Clinton criticized Bush on the campaign trail for the

Gulf War's decisive display of military might yet indecisive ultimate end. With economic difficulties in the fore for most voters, one widely disseminated anti-Bush bumper sticker combined his two reelection difficulties: "Saddam Hussein Still Has a Job...Do You?" Margaret Thatcher, herself dispatched from office by British voters in 1990, found little comfort in the irony of the Gulf War's defeated leader outlasting his antagonists. "There is the aggressor, Saddam Hussein, still in power. There is the President of the United States, no longer in power. There is the Prime Minister of Britain, who did quite a lot to get things there, no longer in power. I wonder who won?"[63]

Clearly any simplistic effort to gauge victory and defeat in the Gulf War merely by who remained standing at its end proves insufficient as a calculus, leading once more to the lingering sense of unfulfilled promise, a generation and yet another war in Iraq later. Indeed emblematic of a shift in American thinking, especially by the oft-termed neoconservative moment that grew in numbers and strength during the 1990s, ultimately grasping control of American policymaking in the immediate aftermath of September 11, 2001, was the transformation of policymakers such as Wolfowitz. As noted above, in 1990 he cared most about American access to oil and the stability of global markets. By the late 1990s, Hussein's place as an immoral leader in opposition to American and global norms was instead paramount in his mind, and sufficient to warrant the Iraqi's disposal. "Saddam has been compared often to Hitler, people say too often," he testified to Congress in 1998. "I think he's better compared to Stalin. Hitler ruled by many means; terror was only one of them. For Stalin, terror was the beginning and the end, and for Saddam terror is the beginning and the end. Many of the calculations that we find irrational are calculations meant to terrorize people, including his closest associates. He trusts no one around him, and for very good reason." This was a man who had forsaken his moral authority to rule, Wolfowitz argued, though he charged the Clinton Administration lacked the moral purpose or political will to "liberate ourselves, our friends and allies in the region, and the Iraqi people themselves from the menace of Saddam Hussein." Oil, by 1998, was less Wolfowitz's public concern.[64]

In the final analysis, and as the chapters that follow clearly demonstrate, the Gulf War cannot adequately be explained as merely a conflict between states, neither as regional conflict, nor merely one for oil. As historian Lawrence Freedman persuasively argues in his contribution to this volume, larger historical narratives were at hand. The Gulf War was also a vestige of colonialism, while for Richard Haass it revealed the wisdom of American policymaking when conducted out of necessity, and by extension the folly of American decision making when prompted less by strategic necessity and instead more by moral choice. Michael Gordon ably demonstrates that the Gulf War also illustrated, for its proponents in any event, a new revolution in military affairs, though one that revealed anew the sheer disparity of power ingrained in East-West and colonial relations for centuries far longer than the Cold War ever lingered, a point reinforced by Shibley Telhami's thorough study of the war's impact on Arab political thinking then and later.

Connecting each of these interpretations are questions of stability and change. The Cold War's end eroded the most stabilizing factor within the international system since 1945, even if superpower tensions threatened at times the ultimate annihilation of the entire globe. What came after the Cold War was less globally dangerous, yet in a real sense more terrifying, as conflict—be it produced by ethnicity, oil, ideology, morality, or a simplistic desire to promote political change through fear and terror—appeared at once more random yet more pervasive. Even the United States itself, long-distanced from international troubles by virtue of its ocean moats, suffered direct assault in the unstable new world order. The Gulf War provided a template for leaders to envision and describe what they hoped might occur after 1989; the Gulf War, as it actually played out, with recurrent superpower tension and the international community's inability to eliminate a tyrant short of absolute conquest of his people and lands, demonstrated that the future offered promise, but that history itself was unlikely to disappear anytime soon. Twenty years on, the same conclusion holds.

[2]

THE GULF WAR: ITS PLACE IN HISTORY

Richard N. Haass

Two decades is little more than a moment when it comes to history. So making an assessment of the Gulf War (sometimes referred to as the first Iraq war) may seem premature to some. Making the assessment even more difficult is that this chapter is being written amidst truly convulsive events taking place in the Middle East, including in Iraq itself. All this is not grounds for avoiding analysis, as policymakers and others do not have the luxury of holding off dealing with today's challenges until the lessons from yesterday's are clear. But it does argue for undertaking this assessment with a large dose of humility and caution, in particular when it comes to drawing conclusions that are either large or meant to last.

As will become apparent, the assessment here is that the Gulf War constituted a significant historical milestone. That said, it did not bring peace or stability to the volatile Middle East, alter the world's dependence upon oil, or usher in an era of either prolonged American dominance or global consensus on the rules of international relations and how they were to be conducted. But had the Gulf War not been fought and fought successfully, it would likely have brought about an era of far greater insecurity and conflict.

Sometimes policymakers need to be recognized less for what they created than for what they averted. This is one of those times.

THE BACKDROP TO WAR

Many of the basic facts surrounding the Gulf War are widely known and broadly if not universally accepted. The Iraqi invasion of Kuwait in August 1990 caught most policymakers—including this one (I was the senior Middle East hand on the staff of the National Security Council at the time)—as a surprise until it was imminent. The prevailing view within the administration of George H. W. Bush was that Iraq was too exhausted from its long war with Iran to undertake any new aggressive action of this sort and would focus instead on rebuilding its economy and infrastructure. There was even hope that Iraq might be prepared to reintegrate itself into the region on pragmatic, responsible terms. (The Arab Cooperation Council was created in large part for this purpose.) Toward this end, the Bush Administration did try for about a year to build a relationship with Saddam Hussein's government. It was a classic experiment in "constructive engagement," an attempt in this case to build on the limited cooperation that grew up between the two governments during the years of the Iran-Iraq war, when the United States provided some assistance to Iraq in order to counter Iran, which was seen as the greater threat to US interests in the region. But this effort by the Bush Administration had already come to naught by the spring of 1990 when a number of actions and statements by Saddam Hussein and his government made clear that he had little interest in improved relations with the United States.

In any event, most US government analysts and officials judged that the Iraqi military buildup along the Kuwaiti border in July

1990 was a modern-day version of gunboat diplomacy, something designed to coerce Kuwait into forgiving Iraqi debt and abiding by OPEC output quotas so that oil production would fall and prices would presumably rise. (Iraq was clearly desperate at the time for increased revenues so that Saddam could rebuild and rearm, although the degree of this desperation was just as clearly underestimated by most outsiders.) Friendly Arab governments interpreted events and likely Iraqi behavior in just this fashion, and cautioned the United States not to "overreact" to the Iraqi military buildup lest it undermine ongoing diplomatic efforts intended to defuse Iraqi-Kuwait tensions or even trigger a conflict that otherwise would not occur. Just to be clear: those of us in the administration recognized that Iraq had the capacity to overwhelm Kuwait militarily; we just did not believe it would choose to do so. But as is almost always the case in the intelligence realm, intentions are more difficult to divine than capabilities.

In the end, Saddam Hussein invaded and annexed Kuwait, in large part because he needed its oil revenues and because he thought he could get away with it. He had contempt for his fellow Arabs, understood that Kuwait was loathed by many of its neighbors, and may well have calculated that the United States and the world would learn to live with the new status quo even if they never learned to like it.

Some have subsequently argued that the United States could (and should) have done more to deter the Iraqi aggression. In fact, there was much back and forth within the administration in mid-July about how to reduce the odds (generally judged to be low) that Iraq's mobilization would lead to an outbreak of fighting. The State Department declared on July 18 that the United States "remained determined to ensure the free flow of oil through the Strait of Hormuz and to defend the principle of freedom of navigation. We also remain strongly committed to supporting the individual and collective self-defense of our friends in the Gulf with whom we have deep and longstanding ties." What made it particularly difficult to take a tougher line toward Iraq (in addition to skepticism about Saddam's real intentions) was pressure on the United States from Arab governments not to do too much to warn Baghdad or prepare for the worst lest such actions by the United States actually contribute to a momentum toward war. Kuwait turned down an offer to participate in a military exercise that would demonstrate its ties to the United States and US willingness and ability to work with it. The only exception to this reticence came from the United Arab Emirates, which on July 22 asked that the United States dispatch aerial refueling tankers and exercise with its air force. Over the objections of the Saudis and others, the Bush Administration quickly agreed, although a week later I found out that the exercise had not taken place as designed because the US tankers and UAE planes could not "mate."

Then, on July 25, US Ambassador to Iraq April Glaspie received word that she had been summoned to meet Saddam. This had never happened before, and the short notice made it impossible for her to receive formal instructions. She was widely criticized for her performance in the meeting and for not doing more to signal to Iraq that any aggression on its part would be firmly and decisively rebuffed, but much of this criticism was unfair. In particular, observers took one statement out of context—that the United States took "no position" on the territorial dispute between Iraq and Kuwait—and interpreted it to mean that this country did not care if Iraq used force against Kuwait. Glaspie's point (one that was clear from a reading of the transcript of the entire meeting) was to underscore that the United States did not hold a position on where borders ought to be drawn but that the United States "can never excuse settlement of disputes by other than peaceful means." What is more, amidst a rambling monologue filled with bluster, Saddam did communicate his agreement to sit down with the Kuwaitis and find a peaceful settlement to the crisis.

This last point was the bottom line of the ambassador's reporting cable back to Washington. It was consistent with the message being communicated to Washington from Egyptian President Hosni Mubarak and others, and was consistent, too, with our own reading of the situation, namely, that Saddam was deploying much of his army along Iraq's southern border to bully Kuwait. Ambassador Glaspie's cable reporting on her meeting with Saddam came in at the same time the CIA issued a warning of possible war and just as those of us in the government were deliberating what sort of message to send Saddam in order to get him to stand down. The administration was leaning toward something quite muscular. I had sent a memo through National Security Advisor Brent Scowcroft for the President that suggested three possibilities in descending order of likelihood: that Saddam was bluffing, that he was about to grab a piece of Kuwait to trade for financial help, or that he was actually contemplating an invasion and possible conquest. The memo went on to urge that the President send the sternest of warnings to Saddam and back up those words with highly visible military actions. But after reading Glaspie's report from Baghdad, I pulled the memo back, believing it was no longer necessary and that more assertive actions along the lines I advocated risked being counterproductive given the apparent shift in the crisis in the direction of a diplomatic resolution. Things looked good enough that Ambassador Glaspie left Baghdad on a long-scheduled vacation.

The message we did send from the President to Saddam on July 28 was meant to be calming but with an underlying message of strength. It referred back to Saddam's meeting three days before with Ambassador Glaspie and to a meeting he had held earlier that spring with a visiting American congressional delegation led by Republican Senator Bob Dole:

> I was pleased to learn of the agreement between Iraq and Kuwait to begin negotiations in Jeddah to find a peaceful solution to the current tensions between you. The United States and Iraq both have a strong interest in preserving the peace and stability of the Middle East. For this reason, we believe that differences are best resolved by peaceful means and not by threats involving military force or conflict. I also welcome your statement that Iraq desires friendship rather than confrontation with the United States. Let me reassure you, as my ambassador, Senator Dole, and others have done, that my administration continues to desire better relations with Iraq. We will also continue to support our friends in the region with whom we have had long-standing ties. We see no necessary inconsistency between these two objectives...

Both Ambassador Glaspie and the administration were criticized after the fact for not having done more to convince Saddam Hussein not to attack. I do not believe that, under the circumstances, there was more we could or should have done or, more fundamentally, that anything we might have done would have made a difference. Saddam was a selective reader of history, and it is clear from his July 25 meeting with Glaspie that he viewed the United States as soft. This was the lesson he took from Vietnam and, more recently and closer to home, from the American withdrawal from Lebanon in 1984 following the bombing of the marine barracks there. To be sure, statements by various administration officials that we had no formal alliance commitment to Kuwait were unfortunate and may have reinforced these perceptions. And nearly all of us were wrong in discounting the possibility that Saddam might invade Kuwait as he did. Still, on any number of occasions the United States signaled its commitment to its friends, and US forces remained in the region to underscore that commitment. There was no way the ambassador or anyone else could have credibly threatened Saddam with a response on the scale of what the United States and the world ultimately did in the Gulf War. It is also important to keep in mind Saddam's lack of respect for his fellow Arabs. He almost certainly dismissed the possibility that they would rally around Kuwait (widely disliked for the arrogant way its officials were often perceived) and stand up to him. I am also reminded of the small sign that Bob Gates (then the Deputy National Security Advisor) kept on his desk: "The best way to achieve complete strategic surprise is to take an action that is either stupid or completely contrary to your self-interest."

In any event, just three days later, a Saudi-hosted meeting between Iraq and Kuwait produced nothing. Over those same days, the Iraqi buildup and mobilization continued unabated. On the morning of August 1, Charlie Allen, the National Intelligence Officer for Warning, again came to see me. This time I was persuaded the Iraqis were doing more than intimidation; military action looked highly likely. The intelligence community sounded the alarm, upgrading its "warning of war" to a more imminent "warning of attack." An interagency meeting was hastily convened on the State Department's seventh floor. By late afternoon, I returned to the White House with the mission of persuading Brent Scowcroft and the President to make one last attempt to dissuade Saddam Hussein from making good on his threat to attack Kuwait. Saddam did just that while we were discussing the mechanics of how best to reach him.

Initial American policy in the aftermath of the invasion was marked by more than a little improvisation, as there was no playbook or diplomatic contingency plan to fall back on. Within days, though, the US response to the invasion had become both explicit and unequivocal: Iraq's aggression against Kuwait must be undone, immediately, completely, and unconditionally. President Bush summed up this position succinctly on the White House lawn upon his return via helicopter from Camp David that first Sunday of the crisis, telling the assembled reporters and the world: "This will not stand." This was the essence of UN Security Council Resolution 660, the baseline statement by the international community passed only hours after the Iraqi invasion.

In the war's aftermath this willingness and ability by the Bush Administration to resist and ultimately reverse Iraq's aggression was discounted by many observers, in part I would argue because so much was accomplished at a relatively small price. I often heard that any American President and administration would have acted similarly. In addition, criticism was aimed at the Bush Administration for not accomplishing even more, that is, the removal of the regime. But this reaction misses an important point, namely, that it was anything but inevitable that the United States would do as much as it in fact did in August 1990 and subsequently. The vote in the Senate on a resolution authorizing US military action against Iraq nearly failed to pass despite Iraq's aggression, reports of its treatment of Kuwaiti nationals, a dozen UN Security Council resolutions, and five months of demonstration of the limits to what draconian economic sanctions backed by force could bring about. A good many voices in the national security debate opposed using force to liberate Kuwait, with many arguing that doing so would prove extraordinarily costly, end in failure, or both.

The point here is that people truly matter. Leadership also truly matters. Little in history is inevitable. It is not at all obvious to me that other occupants of the Oval Office would have made the same decisions that George H. W. Bush and those around him did to amass an unprecedented international coalition and, in the end, oust Iraq from Kuwait by military force. There was no guarantee of success, certainly not at a modest price. It is quite possible others would have satisfied themselves with a decision to defend Saudi Arabia and try to weaken Iraq with sanctions—in effect, opt for Desert Shield but eschew Desert Storm. But this would have been a disastrous course, as it would have given Saddam effective control of the region and its energy and would have placed extraordinary pressure on the Saudis and others, in part because of the need to maintain a large military presence on their territory. It also would have required far more in the way of US military forces than what was needed for containment in the wake of the Gulf War.

There are also some lessons to be learned about sanctions. Sanctions turn out to be an extraordinarily complex foreign policy instrument. As a rule of thumb, their effectiveness increases to the degree they enjoy considerable international backing, are buttressed by military force, and allow for humanitarian exceptions to lessen their impact on innocent civilians. International backing in turn can be increased if essential parties and states are subsidized to offset the costs of compliance. Several of Iraq's neighbors benefited from illegal trade with Iraq in the years after the Gulf War, and more could and should have been done to give them an incentive to comply with sanctions, that is, compensate them for any lost income. But even in ideal circumstances, sanctions tend to be limited in what they can accomplish. They can influence behavior and selected capabilities, but they cannot be expected to produce fundamental changes in actions, capacities, or nature in a limited amount of time. Indeed, in this case, sanctions could not force Saddam Hussein to leave Kuwait.

What is more, not all that sanctions accomplish is positive, in the sense that they can work against certain policy ends. In the case of Iraq, sanctions actually made it less difficult for Saddam Hussein to maintain control at home while they created sympathy for him and his country abroad. Still, sanctions coupled with inspections and select applications of military force did help to contain Saddam to a considerable degree—and arguably could have accomplished even more if everything that could have been done had been done to strengthen them. It is worth noting that this example of the limits of sanctions does not seem to have dissuaded subsequent administrations from relying on them to try to produce major policy changes from targeted governments such as those that control North Korea and Iran.

THE WAR AND ITS AFTERMATH

US policy unfolded in several stages in the wake of Iraq's occupation of Kuwait. The first, Desert Shield, sought at a minimum to stabilize the situation, that is, to deter further Iraqi aggression, in this instance against Saudi Arabia, the country with the largest proven reserves of oil in the world. It also sought to put into place those military assets that would be required if policies other than a resort to force, including diplomacy and economic sanctions, failed to bring about Iraqi compliance with UN Security Council Resolution 660. Toward these and related ends, the United States put together an extraordinary international coalition of dozens of countries, some providing troops, others access to facilities or overflight rights, and still others financial support.

Some 500,000 American troops were ultimately dispatched to the region, where they were joined by another 200,000 soldiers from other countries.

The second stage of post-invasion US policy was Desert Storm, initiated in mid-January 1991, after five and a half months of unsuccessful efforts to engineer a complete and unconditional Iraqi withdrawal from Kuwait. Desert Storm was relatively short: it took only some six weeks of air war followed by four days of ground action. The results of Desert Storm were impressive and then some by any measure. Kuwait was in fact liberated in full and without condition and restored to its rulers and people. Iraq's armed forces were seriously downgraded—although not so completely that Iraq could not constitute something of a balance to Iran, still very much a strategic threat in American eyes. That all this was accomplished in some seven weeks of combat was extraordinary. The war cost less than 200 American lives and less than $100 billion—and virtually all of this economic cost was offset by cash or in-kind payments received from members of the international coalition. It was all a testament to the skill of American diplomacy—and even more to the servicemen and women and to their ability to take advantage of intelligence and technology.

What was avoided by the defeat of Iraq was Iraqi primacy over the oil and gas rich Middle East. An Iraq in possession of all of Kuwait's financial and mineral resources would have become not just "a" but "the" dominant local power. (Together, Iraq and Kuwait amount to some 20% of the region's reserves.) Iraq would not have needed to be in physical control of its neighbors' territory or resources in order to have been in a position to have exercised tremendous influence over them. It is no exaggeration to say that the US-led action precluded what would otherwise have led to the "Finlandization" of Saudi Arabia, which would have been independent in name only. Iraq would have been far more powerful, and the demonstration of what happened to Kuwait when it did not do what Iraq wanted would have been lost on no one in Riyadh. Iraq would have been in a far stronger position to influence and possibly dictate policies affecting oil availability and price. It would also, we now know, have been likely to gain nuclear weapons within years.

There would have been other undesirable effects of a failure to reverse Iraq's aggression. Iraq would have become the dominant Arab state. It likely would have set back the chances of negotiating peace between Israel and its neighbors unless Saddam Hussein for some reason decided that was something he wanted. This would have been highly unlikely given Saddam's desire for Arab leadership. It is not clear the Israel-Jordan peace accord could or would have been negotiated in such a context. A dominant Iraq also would have complicated US efforts to work with selected local governments against terrorism, a critical US foreign policy consideration.

An Iraq in control of Kuwait and its oil that was able to develop nuclear weapons would have stimulated further nuclear proliferation, most obviously in Iran. Iran has gone down this path in any event, although it can be argued that it would have done so more quickly with a clear Iraqi threat and that it would have been difficult if not impossible to muster international opposition to an Iranian nuclear program as it would have been seen as an understandable (and, in some quarters, desirable) response to an Iraqi capability. Other regional countries, including Egypt, Turkey, and Saudi Arabia, would have been tempted to follow suit, likely resulting in a Middle East with multiple fingers on multiple nuclear triggers, a recipe for disaster if there ever was one.

It is important, too, to underscore what was accomplished indirectly by US policy. "International community" is a phrase commonly invoked when in reality there is little or no community of thought or action. Yet in this instance there were both. Support was near universal in the aftermath of Saddam's invasion and absorption of Kuwait for the principle that military force is not to be used to change borders or, in this case, to eliminate countries. This, after all, was the fundamental rule of world order that had informed international relations for some three and a half centuries. That this rule was upheld only months after the crumbling of the Berlin Wall at the end of one historical era and the dawn of another was particularly important, as it set an important precedent. It is impossible to know what other countries would have acted aggressively had Iraq been allowed to get away with what it did, but odds are appeasement of Saddam would have sent a powerful message that aggression pays. Most likely it would have been replicated elsewhere.

Some other positives are worth noting as well. The success in the Persian Gulf helped ease the transition at the end of the Cold War for the Soviet Union. It suggested that a partnership of sorts with the United States was possible. US-Soviet cooperation also suggested the potential for a new role for the United Nations, as Soviet protection (and, if need be, a veto in the Security Council) was no longer something to be assumed by countries that had long enjoyed Soviet support. This same reality, though, had a less positive result: a looser international system, one no longer defined by a Cold War in which the two superpowers could exert considerable influence or even a degree of control over their clients and allies, was one in which medium-sized states and others could make decisions and take actions that never would have been tolerated in a more structured system. Saddam Hussein's act of aggression was something of a harbinger of a less disciplined international future.

At the same time, it was and is important to take note of what was not accomplished, some longer term costs, and the limits to the war's success. There is the obvious fact that Saddam managed to hang on to power. This was unexpected, as almost everyone involved in US policymaking at the time assumed he would not be able to politically survive such a catastrophic defeat. What may well have saved him were the twin rebellions within Iraq that followed the war, as these provided an opportunity to Saddam to rally his Sunni base and to present himself as the defender of Iraq's unity. The war also failed to destroy much of Iraq's weapons of mass destruction capacity, including three different uranium enrichment programs that survived the war.

As for longer term costs, there were the direct military and economic expense that stemmed from the decision to station troops and aircraft in the region to enforce no-fly zones over Iraq that were intended to limit Saddam's ability to repress his own people. Forces were also kept in the region to protect Kuwait and Saudi Arabia from any new Iraqi aggression. This obviously constituted something of a military and economic drain on the United States. A possible indirect cost of the need to keep military forces in Saudi Arabia was that it alienated and humiliated some Saudis and others; indeed, this presence was one of the reasons Osama Bin Laden gave for al-Qaeda's existence, that is, to rid the country of foreign, non-Moslem people. This alleged motivation should not be exaggerated, though, given the radicalism of al-Qaeda's agenda. It is more than likely Bin Laden and others would have found ample reason to attack the United States on 9/11 and on other occasions even if no American soldier had ever set foot on the Arabian Peninsula.

The fact that Saddam survived Desert Storm and fought back against uprisings in both Iraq's south and north led to two humanitarian crises, one that required substantial outside inter-vention. This, too, was partly a result of what Desert Storm did not accomplish. But the costs of this inaction need to be weighed against the potential costs of what would have been associated with an American effort to oust Saddam and put something and someone substantially better in his place. It is always difficult to consider alternative histories, but here at least there is one indica-tion of the potential costs of such a policy, namely, the 2003 Iraq war, which did "march on Baghdad," oust Saddam Hussein, and aim to insert something better in his regime's place. The costs of this policy included more than 4,000 American lives, as much as a trillion dollars, and considerable diplomatic and political alien-ation. Even without such costs, and as the Middle East upheavals of 2011 demonstrate, it is also not at all certain that a successor government would have emerged that was clearly to our liking.

The decision to stop the war when it was stopped and not to go to Baghdad in an effort to oust the regime was a considered one. The President was motivated by a desire to maintain domes-tic and international support for the coalition and its mission. He liked the idea of pressing for peace before it was pressed on him and staying one step ahead of calls from coalition governments and Democrats at home that we cease operations. This would be a way to bank goodwill with the Soviets and Arabs in particular—goodwill that would come in handy if and when the United States turned its attention to the Middle East peace process and other regional challenges. The American military leadership seemed particularly uncomfortable with the "turkey shoot" quality of its continued pursuit and killing of poorly armed and trained Iraqi troops, many of whom were conscripts. There was a sense that the wrong people were dying, something that would not help rebuild Iraq and that would hurt America's image. (I voiced my sense that we were appearing to "pile on," an analogy drawn from American football when tacklers hit an opposing player already down on the ground.) There was also the strategic rationale, that is, that the United States wanted an Iraq still strong enough to offset the latent desire of Iran to bid for regional primacy. And there was a desire to avoid more American casualties that were sure to result from continued fighting.

What also colored the thinking of people in the administration was the information (incorrect as it turned out) that coalition forces had essentially trapped several of the better-trained and equipped Iraqi Republican Guard divisions, who would be forced to leave their equipment behind or risk being attacked. What the Prussian military strategist Carl Von Clausewitz termed the "fog of war" was in effect that day. The cuteness of stopping at 100 hours may have affected the timing by a few hours but not more. My own sense at the time (it was actually my assumption up to that morning) was that the US-led coalition could and should carry on the war for one or two more days. I believe we could have done so without endangering either the coalition or our image, and if we had done so, could have weakened Iraqi forces more than we did and further humiliated Saddam. Whether all this would have changed his ability to weather his failure to hold Kuwait and survive the subsequent rebellions is simply unknown.

The truth is there was no interest in going to Baghdad and forcibly removing Saddam. I do not recall any dissent on this point. The consensus was that the United States would lose more troops in such an operation than we had lost up to that point. The Bush Administration had also just had the frustrating experience of going after Manuel Noriega in Panama; searching modern cities for individuals is dangerous and difficult work. Such operations did not play to the advantage of American forces, which did best in open battlefields where mobility, technology, and advanced arms could all be brought to bear in an integrated fashion. A march to Baghdad would have gone beyond the terms of relevant UN Security Council and congressional resolutions, all of which posed not so much legal considerations as political ones. Bush felt he had made a pact with the rest of the world and he did not want to break it and in the process diminish trust in American commitments. He and we feared that the coalition would shatter if the United States pressed its objectives beyond what had been stated at the outset. There was also the belief that what we had accomplished would create an environment in which Saddam was unlikely to survive. The shared prediction was that the defeated Iraqi military would turn on him in retribution for his recklessness. This prediction also provided a justification for not expressly requiring Saddam's removal as a precondition for ending the war even though he had torched Kuwait's oil wells—an act that crossed a US red line and was meant to trigger actions designed to bring about his ouster.

One historical analogy that influenced several policymakers in the Bush Administration at this juncture was Korea. More specifically, what came to mind was the decision to march north of the 38th parallel. Douglas MacArthur pushed for and President Harry S. Truman signed off on expanded US war objectives in the flush of tactical success following his inspired landing at Inchon. He had liberated all of the South and restored the status quo ante. But not content to leave it at that, he continued north. Neither China nor the Soviet Union was prepared to allow the entire country to be in the American orbit. Hundreds of thousands of Chinese "volunteers" joined with the North Koreans to push back. Three years and 30,000 American lives later, the United States accepted an armistice based on a division of Korea at the same 38th parallel. This was a classic case of mission creep—or, more accurately, mission leap—with an immense human, military, economic, and diplomatic cost. I had taught (with Professor Ernest May) the course at the Kennedy School based on the wonderful book *Thinking in Time* that he had coauthored with Richard Neustadt on the use and misuse of history for decision makers. Of course, there were differences between the Korea of 1951 and the Iraq of 1991, but so, too, were there parallels to be seen and lessons to be drawn. Yes, it was tempting to allow US objectives to change from liberating Kuwait to liberating Iraq, especially given how well the war had gone to that point. But as is often the case in life, temptation is best resisted.

The policy of not intervening directly to assist those rising up against Saddam Hussein is another set of decisions that has come under considerable scrutiny and, on occasion, substantial criticism. Some background is needed here. As early as the first day of March, there emerged evidence of an uprising—an intifada, the Arabic word for "casting off"—in the south of Iraq dominated by the Shia, a Muslim sect that had long been repressed by Saddam but that constituted at least a plurality and possibly a majority of all Iraqis. The question was what if anything the United States would do. There was a strong disposition not to get involved. General Colin Powell (then Chairman of the Joint Chiefs of Staff) and other senior military leaders stressed that US intervention, which would have involved trying to coordinate military operations with disparate groups of Iraqis against other Iraqis, promised to be an operational nightmare. Telling the good guys from the bad—identifying friend from foe in military parlance—would be all but impossible. There was also deep concern about the political goals and orientation of Iraq's Shia. What worried me and others was Iran's actual and potential sway—concerns, I would argue, that have been shown to have been legitimate in light of Iran's substantial influence in post-Saddam Iraq.

A few days later, in early March, another intifada broke out in the north of Iraq between the Kurds and Sunni-dominated, Iraqi-government forces. Again, there was no US military intervention. Intervention in the north on behalf of the Kurds, who wanted nothing so much as their own independent country, would have not just alienated Turkey but triggered a war with it. Kurdish independence was unacceptable to the Turks, who feared it would lead to the breakup of their own country given the attraction an independent "Kurdistan" would hold for Turkey's sizable Kurdish minority. The subsequent humanitarian operation undertaken that spring by the United States to assist the massive number of Iraqi Kurds who had headed north to escape Saddam's attacks was just that—humanitarian—and was not designed or implemented to advance Kurdish separatism or statehood.

It was in between these two outbreaks that a meeting was hastily arranged between the coalition military leadership and their Iraqi military counterparts in the Iraqi city of Safwan, located just north of the Kuwaiti border. General Norman Schwarzkopf was determined to avoid the twin extremes of either humiliating the Iraqis or being overly nice, recounting in his memoir that he explicitly told Prince Khalid, the commander of Saudi Arabia's armed forces, "Please, none of this 'Arab brother' business when the Iraqis arrive. No embracing or kissing each other on both cheeks." The Safwan meeting was seen mostly as dealing with minor, technical issues, so much so that the US military drafted its own instructions.

A lot has been said and written about why the United States did not do more to stop Saddam's crackdowns in the south and north of Iraq. Many point to Schwarzkopf's decision at Safwan to allow the Iraqis to resume helicopter flights for administrative purposes such as supplying troops—only to have the Iraqis use helicopters instead to crush the rebellions. It is true that the US military representatives made this decision, but it is not fair to hold them responsible for what ensued. This was no time to be reluctant to overrule the commander in the field. Those around the President could and arguably should have pressed to rescind this permission, and the President could have so ordered. But, even had he done so, doing this would not have solved the problem. We then would have faced the need to impose the decision to ban Iraqi helicopter flights or to act with force if and when the Iraqis turned to other weapons to defeat those in opposition to the government. There was no reason to believe only helicopters would prove decisive. Schwarzkopf makes just this point in his memoir: "[G]rounding the helicopter gunships would have had little impact. The tanks and artillery of the twenty-four Iraqi divisions that never entered the Kuwaiti war zone were having a far more devastating effect on the insurgents." Many of us in Washington viewed reversing the helicopter decision as starting down a slippery and dangerous slope that would have risked a quagmire.

Still, it must be said that US policymaking during this period was ragged. There is simply no other word for it. There was a natural and perhaps understandable but no less unfortunate loss of focus and letting up after seven months of nonstop crisis. There had been a good deal of planning for the postwar period, but not for internal Iraq scenarios such as we were seeing given the policy decision that the international coalition and the United States in particular would not become an occupying power or try to recast the internal politics of a defeated Iraq. Again, the operating assumption was that a disenchanted Iraqi military, still the most powerful force in the country, would likely oust Saddam and find someone else to lead Iraq in the "Arab way," that is, an authoritarian, Sunni-dominated state, but one without Saddam's excesses, which had led to two wars in the region in a decade and severe repression at home. Like most assumptions, this was based not on hard evidence but on a mixture of assessment and prediction—gut feelings or "gut-int" in intelligence lingo.

Much of March and April 1991 played out against the backdrop of the deteriorating situation on the ground in Iraq. The Bush Administration was getting hammered in the press, with comparisons drawn to both 1956 (when the Eisenhower Administration was blamed for inspiring the Hungarian uprising only to do nothing about it when it materialized) and 1961 (when the Kennedy Administration organized and then half-heartedly backed the ill-fated attempt to overthrow Castro that ended up in disaster at the Bay of Pigs). The comparisons were badly overdrawn. Not all historical comparisons are apt. The rebellions in Iraq were not organized, coordinated, or funded in any way by the United States. Some people may have expected that the United States would assist them, but no word had been passed or commitment given. The President's calls for the Iraqi people to overthrow Saddam were mostly made in the context of avoiding coalition military activity, that is, if you oust Saddam, you will escape getting attacked by the international community when it moves to implement the relevant Security Council resolutions.

ASSESSING THE WAR

What, then, can be said about the Gulf War? The response to Saddam Hussein's aggression was undertaken by an unprecedented international coalition, including the two principal protagonists of the just-concluded Cold War and several Arab countries. Nevertheless, one should not exaggerate the degree of "international community" that emerged from the war. Agreement on one principle of international relations (in this case, the right of states to act in their own self-defense along with the right of others to assist them) should not be confused with a common definition of what constitutes international order. Subsequent years and developments demonstrated that international consensus on preventing genocide, stopping nuclear proliferation, or thwarting terrorism, trade protectionism, or climate change was thin or nonexistent. The first Iraq war constituted an important moment in world history, but not a transformation.

The judgment that this first war with Iraq qualified as a success derived from the fact that the principal war aims (the reversal of Iraqi aggression and the restoration to power of the Kuwaiti government) were accomplished. That both aims were realized at only modest human, economic, and military cost to the United States and to great domestic and international applause only reinforces the judgment that what the United States did constituted a success. It is also worth noting that the first Iraq war is consistent with the precepts of the just war: it was fought for a worthy cause, it was likely to succeed, it was undertaken with legitimate authority, and it was waged only as a last resort.

This is not to suggest that the first Iraq war should be viewed as a textbook case of how to conduct foreign policy. The administration of George H. W. Bush misread Iraqi intentions; more could have been done (although it is impossible to know with what effect) to deter an invasion. US intelligence badly underestimated just how much work Iraq had done on weapons of mass destruction. The end of the war also could have been better handled. More of the Iraqi army should have been bottled up and either disarmed or destroyed. Signals to the Iraqi population about what the United States was and was not prepared to do should have been made clearer. More could have been done sooner to lessen the humanitarian tragedy. But the critics go too far. For one thing, failing to reverse Saddam's aggression would have set a terrible precedent and led to a host of adverse effects in a critical region of the world. For another, it remains uncertain and even unlikely that US policy could have brought about Saddam Hussein's ouster and replacement by someone and something markedly better at a reasonable cost.

It may be useful in this context to compare and contrast the Gulf War with the second Iraq war.

- The first was a limited, in many ways traditional war, one that sought to reverse Iraq's external aggression and restore the status quo ante; the second was an ambitious, even radical, initiative designed to oust and replace Iraq's leadership and, in so doing, create the foundations for a very different Middle East.
- The first war was essentially reactive and consistent with the universally accepted doctrine of self-defense; the second was a case of preventive war that enjoyed far less legal underpinning and political support.
- The first Iraq war was a truly multilateral affair, with dozens of countries ranging from Russia and Japan to Egypt and Syria forming an unprecedented international coalition and contributing in ways both varied (diplomatic, military, economic) and significant; the second war was for all intents and purposes unilateral, with the United States supported meaningfully by Great Britain and few others.
- The first Iraq war came about after more than a dozen UN Security Council resolutions failed to dislodge Saddam from Kuwait. The second war was launched with the

backing of one new UN Security Council resolution and after the United States concluded it could not gain support for a second.

- For the first Iraq war, the United States went to the United Nations for backing that the administration believed would make it less difficult to build domestic and above all congressional support for using armed force; for the second war, the United States went to Congress first and then sought UN authorization.

- The first war made use of some 450,000 US troops and was premised on the Powell Doctrine's bias toward employing overwhelming military force; the second war was designed by Defense Secretary Donald Rumsfeld to minimize the number of US armed forces (approximately 150,000) committed to the effort.

- The first Iraq war began with a prolonged phase in which airpower alone was used by the United States; the second war involved US ground forces early on.

- The first war took place against the backdrop of a "false negative," in which most intelligence analysts and policymakers believed (incorrectly as it turned out) that Saddam would not invade Kuwait; the second war took place against the backdrop of a "false positive," in which most intelligence analysts and policymakers believed (again incorrectly) that Saddam was hiding weapons of mass destruction. Indeed, in the run up to the first war, the United States and the international community placed relatively little emphasis on weapons of mass destruction, although it later became clear that the world had badly underestimated the scale of Iraq's programs; in the run up to the second Iraq war, the administration of George W. Bush placed considerable emphasis on weapons of mass destruction, although it later became clear that US officials had badly overestimated Iraqi capabilities.

- Those who opposed the first Iraq war underestimated the costs of allowing the status quo to stand and overestimated the costs of going to war to evict Iraq from Kuwait; those who favored the second Iraq war underestimated the costs of going to war and overestimated the costs of allowing the status quo to stand.

- The first Iraq war proved to be controversial at home at the outset but ended up being wildly popular; the second Iraq war was initiated with broad congressional and public backing but over time became widely unpopular.

- The first Iraq war cost less than $100 billion and, because of the contributions of coalition states, cost the US government next to nothing. The second war has cost the United States as much as one trillion dollars and possibly (depending on the accounting) considerably more. The tab is still rising and there is no chance of getting anyone to share more than a modest piece of it if that.

- The first war claimed under 200 American lives; the latter more than 4,000.

- The first Iraq war was a classic war of necessity; vital interests were at stake, and only military force could protect them. The second Iraq war was a war of choice. US interests were decidedly less-than-vital, and there were alternative policies other than military force that could have been employed to protect those interests.

What, then, is one to make of the Gulf War now that two decades have passed? It was a war the United States was correct to fight and one that was largely fought correctly. That said, the Gulf

War was significant but not transformational. It was and remains more important for what it prevented than for what it accomplished or brought about. Had it not been waged it could have been transformational, but in the negative sense, ushering in an era of Middle Eastern politics and international relations far more violent that what has transpired.

What made the war less than transformational were three things. The first was what led to it: the Iraqi invasion of Kuwait. This sort of cross-border, state-on-state aggression is no longer the defining threat to international order. What we see instead are two sorts of dominant threats: on one hand, global phenomena ranging from terrorism, the proliferation of weapons of mass destruction, and trade protectionism to pandemic disease and climate change, and on the other, humanitarian and strategic problems that stem from developments within states, including governments who declare war on their own citizens or who are unable to protect or otherwise provide for their own people. The Gulf War was and is something of an exception in an era in which greater threats to order stem either from various transnational or global actors and forces or from what happens within the boundaries of states.

Second, the Gulf War represented the high-water mark of American primacy in the world. The conflict came in the immediate aftermath of the Cold War and in a world no longer dominated by two superpower rivals. But the unipolarity that replaced bipolarity turned out to be short-lived. The rise of Asia and large parts of the rest of the world meant that the US share of global economic output was falling. New global forces and flows (benign and malign alike) were emerging that were beyond the capacity of the United States or any single country to manage. The United States further accelerated the arrival of a world characterized by multiple sources of power (what I have termed "nonpolarity") by costly overseas ventures (in particular the second Iraq war) and by its failure to maintain anything resembling fiscal balance. The Gulf War represented a moment of American dominance that did not last. By contrast, transformations are made of realities that do.

Third, and consistent with the above, the Gulf War was less than transformational because of the lack of follow-up. What I am alluding to is not the decision to avoid intervening in the two post-conflict rebellions or to eschew pushing directly for regime change; as has been discussed, all of these decisions can be justified. Rather, the lack of follow-up reflects what was not accomplished in the way of promoting peace between Israel and the Palestinians, doing more to bring about political and economic reform within Arab countries, reducing US and world dependence on oil, or building consensus and creating the institutions that would in effect have constituted a new world order. These were acts of omission, not commission, and had nothing to do with the diplomacy or conduct of the war itself. They reflected weaknesses of US domestic and foreign policy that spanned several administrations, Republicans and Democrats alike. The Gulf War itself, however, was an important accomplishment, one that should not be underestimated because many of the opportunities it created went unrealized.

[3]

THE INTERNATIONAL POLITICS
OF THE GULF WAR

Lawrence Freedman

The Persian Gulf War came at a transitional moment in international history and was part of that transition. It was shaped by the past while suggesting, erroneously as it turned out, how the future might unfold. Although presented as the first act of a new world order, in practice it was more the last act of an old world order that was coming to a close with more grace and credit than could possibly have been anticipated in advance. The first move in the crisis, when Iraq occupied Kuwait in August 1990, was not long after the fall of a succession of East European communist regimes. In November 1989 the Berlin Wall was breached. The next month at the summit between Presidents George H. W. Bush and Mikhail Gorbachev, conducted on a boat moored in choppy waters off Malta, the Cold War began to be spoken of in the past tense. It had lasted, as Gorbachev's spokesman quipped, "from Yalta to Malta." After the Iraqi invasion but before the Gulf War, with efforts underway to find a peaceful solution to the crisis, the formal end of the Cold War was marked in November 1990 by a conference in Paris to confirm German unification and a new conventional arms control treaty for Europe. In the aftermath of the Gulf War the logic of the collapse of European communism and the delegitimation of Soviet hegemony continued to work through the system with the evaporation of the Warsaw Pact, the relatively orderly dissolution of the Soviet Union (though following a failed coup in Moscow) and the much more bloody dissolution of Yugoslavia.

This conjunction of momentous events makes it difficult to sort out the various influences on the course of international affairs during the subsequent years. We tend to talk of the period that began in 1990 as "post-Cold War" rather than "post-Gulf War," and in terms of what happened over the rest of that decade it is hard to argue. The course of the 1990-91 conflict was certainly shaped by its timing, notably in the roles played by the United States and the Soviet Union and by the United Nations. On the other hand, the next obvious punctuation point in contemporary international history is 9/11, and the events of the decade that has just passed, including the 2003 Iraq War, can clearly be traced back to the aftermath of the war, including the way that it brought the United States much more intimately into the affairs of the Middle East, which aggravated relations with Iran and provided part of the inspiration for the formation of al-Qaeda, and generated divisions in the Security Council over weapons and inspections and sanctions. To some extent all of these events reflected a broader trend, the steady loosening of the colonial ties that had once bound weak states to stronger states, of which the dismantling of the Soviet Empire was a critical step and the buildup to the Gulf War a striking symptom. In the first instance, the manner in which the war was conducted and its satisfactory outcome appeared to have reversed the trend. Over the longer term, the trend has continued.

After World War II, there was a progressive disengagement of the great powers from the areas sometimes known as "the Third World," the "South," or the "developing world." The terms are all misleading for this group of countries lacks an appropriate collective noun. This group had three key features. First, they were previously largely colonized by European powers and began to gain their independence after 1945. This was marked by the expansion of the United Nations from the original 50 members to 192 by 2011. Second, they felt, often with some justice, that they were disadvantaged by international economic and political structures. Most began as primary producers. A number, initially mainly in East Asia, who largely by the 1970s managed to industrialize successfully, moved out of the "developing" status. Those with substantial oil reserves, mainly in the Middle East, conversely acquired wealth without broader industrial development. Those that continued to struggle economically were often also marked by social cleavages and political instability. Third, despite the collective nouns, and entities such as the "nonaligned movement" and the "Group of 77," they never managed to cohere effectively as a group. For developing states, the combination of internal instability and complex regional relations always had the potential for an unpredictable and unruly impact on international affairs.

This impact was at first subdued because of the protracted process of decolonization, the lingering obligations felt by the imperial powers to their former colonies and protectorates, often marked by considerable involvement in their domestic politics, and by the Cold War, which shaped the developing American and Russian engagement in their affairs. It was by way of contrast with the first and second worlds of liberal capitalism and state socialism that the "Third World" was identified. By 1974, with the collapse of the Portuguese empire, the decolonization process was largely complete. As this meant that the imperial powers, with odd exceptions (such as the Falkland Islands), no longer had sovereign interests to defend far from their borders, and the inclination was increasingly to disengage (as in the British withdrawal from "East of Suez" at the end of the 1960s). Instead of taking on security obligations to notionally friendly states, including former colonies, the tendency was to arm them to look after their own security.

|

It could be argued that the end of the Cold War was the reflection of similar processes that animated all decolonization. The yearning for self-determination, first in the Warsaw Pact members of Central and Eastern Europe and then in the republics of the Soviet Union, saw the rapid dismantling of Moscow's continental empire. The sudden evaporation of Soviet power shifted the international balance of power. In the first instance this seemed to open up the possibility of a reassertion of western strength, reflecting liberal capitalism's ideological triumph and the creation of an effective American hegemony. The United States and its allies had not "won" the Cold War because of their military might. There was a view, much encouraged by fans of President Reagan, that the decisive factor was the alarm in the Kremlin about a new conventional arms race in which the Soviets were ill-equipped to compete because of their obsolescent technological base. This factor was not irrelevant, but it only came into play because of the inability of state socialism to compete with the dynamism of liberal capitalism. This was evident in the opening up of global financial markets and trade, on the one hand, which had taken off in the 1980s, and the boost to human rights and democracy as a result of the implosion of European communism, on the other. Soon the talk was of globalization. All countries would soon be subject to the same economic imperatives if they were to prosper and grow, and simplistically it was assumed that these economic perspectives would lead to a uniform political response.

The United States was suddenly in a category of its own, no longer a mere superpower but now a hyperpower. The Soviet Union was suffering relegation. It was only able to maintain a semblance of a great power status because old habits die hard and more fundamentally because it maintained a substantial nuclear inventory. The new configuration of forces and the more relaxed geopolitical setting meant that traditional concerns about the global balance of power appeared to be far less pressing. For the moment the new military relationship between the shrinking Soviet Union and NATO appeared irrelevant. There was uncertainty about whether Russia would continue to present itself as a new friend and partner, but even if it reverted to its old antagonism, the Soviet armed forces were hollowed out, demoralized by the gaping wound that was the unwinnable Soviet intervention in Afghanistan, undermined by the dire state of the economy, and isolated by the collapse of the Warsaw Pact. Central and East European countries now looked to the West. This was the start of the process that would eventually lead to the "Partnership of Peace" and on to full membership of NATO and the European Union.

From Moscow came talk of new international institutional structures, such as a revamped Commission on Security and Cooperation in Europe (CSCE), which would preserve a level of political influence, with a seat at the top table, and neutralize efforts to have new structures that emphasized and consolidated the western triumph. In the face of such proposals, western governments were publically polite but privately dismissive. As it became apparent that it risked being marginalized in Europe, Moscow accepted concessions that allowed it special consultative arrangements with NATO and took to emphasizing the UN

Security Council as a place where its position was unassailable as one of the "permanent five" with veto rights.

The 1990s began in an optimistic mood. The sense of peace-making, which the end of the Cold War encouraged, led to hopes that a range of old animosities that had long vexed international politics, such as apartheid South Africa or the Arab-Israel dispute, or Iranian isolation, might now be addressed productively. Even if there was no progress beyond the end of the Cold War, this on its own justified reductions in force levels. Across NATO the cuts in defense capability tended to be about 25 percent. Indeed there were grounds for wondering whether substantial military establishments would be at all necessary. The end of the Cold War could be presented as the end of the "great power" era, in which the dominant and most pressing security concerns were about whether rival great powers were on the rise and had hegemonic ambitions, and in which the dominant scenario was a major war. Whether or not this was because of the shared fear of a nuclear conflagration, the Cold War had stayed cold. There was concern in the United States about possible "peer competitors" but initially there were no obvious candidates. Germany and Japan were put in the frame in 1990[1] but both stagnated economically during that decade, and it took some time before China started to become taken seriously as anything other than a regional power. Indeed the 1989 suppression of the Tiananmen Square protests had left China somewhat temporarily marginalized. Leaving aside whether any of the potential newcomers were interested in taking on the responsibilities that go with great power status, the struggle for territory that had characterized the great power rivalry for the past was long over. As already noted, the tendency now was in the opposite direction.

Not all, of course, viewed the new situation with optimism. The old guard in Moscow viewed with dismay the unification of the old adversary, Germany, within a NATO alliance that had no intention of following the Warsaw Pact into oblivion. They deplored the collapse of communist discipline and a country in disarray with a contracting economy. In addition, those around the world who had depended on the Soviet Union for arms, military training, and diplomatic backing had to reappraise their position. Socialists were depressed by the retreat of the notions of state planning and regulation and alarmed by the prospect of unfettered capitalism. Nonetheless the overall mood was positive. While President George H. Bush might have been considered slow in acknowledging just how fast and how far events were moving during the course of 1989, once it all became clear his administration moved decisively yet sympathetically to manage the processes of German unification and the effective decline of the Soviet Union. It took time for all this to work itself through the international system, but the broad hopes and expectations of the immediate post-Cold War era provided the background to Iraq's invasion of Kuwait at the start of August 1990.

II

The Middle East was a region of strategic importance, for which read oil, and so one that the major powers dared not neglect. It was also subject to the growing fluidity of international politics and alignments, challenging attempts by all outsiders to influence the course of events. At the start of the 1960s, for example, Britain could still act to prevent Iraq from making a grab for Kuwait. By the end of that decade it had decided to give up on a role "East of Suez." Even if Britain had decided to maintain bases in the region, its position was bound to become increasingly tenuous. Although in the 1950s the Soviet Union made a pitch to catch the tide of history by supporting the more radical, antisocialist secular regimes, of which Nasser's Egypt was the first. Nasser's successor, Anwar Sadat, switched his allegiance to the United States. After the 1967 Arab-Israeli war the French decided to abandon Israel in favor of the same collection of radical states, only making any serious headway with Iraq. Rather than replace Britain as regional arbiter, the United States decided to build up Saudi Arabia and Iran as separate "pillars" to look after western interests in the region. But their interests included a higher oil price. They also had their own long-standing political and religious tensions. Then, at the end of the 1970s Iran turned away from the West following its revolution and allowed its relations with Saudi Arabia to take on the form of a cold war.

For all these reasons, instead of Middle Eastern conflicts being governed by the big strategic contest of the Cold War they increasingly became detached from the Cold War and developed their own trajectories. Both reflecting and accelerating these trends was Iraq. A pro-British monarch was deposed in the 1950s and at first Iraq followed the Nasserite path of close association (short of formal alliance) with the Soviet Union. It then took advantage of overtures from France during the 1970s to develop an alternative supplier of arms and nuclear technology. At the start of the 1980s it went to war with Iran, reflecting traditional Persian-Arab tensions, with an overlay of Shia-Sunni and clerical-secular antagonism. External powers dabbled in this conflict, largely on behalf of Iraq, but a stalemate was not seen as a big problem. With a glut of oil in the 1980s and the oil price at rock bottom, the region seemed less vital than in the previous decade when OPEC states had pushed the price to artificial highs.

This was the context for the Iraqi invasion of Kuwait. The motives could be found in the shared history of Iraq and Kuwait in the old Ottoman Empire, and Iraq's indebtedness to Kuwait as a result of the Iran-Iraq War. A key factor was the collapse in oil price, which had intensified Saddam Hussein's economic predicament, just as it had been an important factor in undermining the Soviet Union. Iraq blamed Kuwait for failing to adhere to OPEC production costs that had been intended to boost prices. For President Saddam Hussein of Iraq the changing configuration of power was also relevant. If the wave of democratization and human rights were to extend into the Middle East, then he was vulnerable. There were stories of videos of the December 1989 summary execution of the Ceauşescus in Romania being circulated around Baghdad. He was also becoming edgy as his nuclear and chemical weapons programs began to attract international attention. The threat to the Iraqi regime posed by its indebtedness was aggravated by the loss of the Soviet Union as a supplier and the increasing unwillingness of the western suppliers to provide credits and their anxieties about weapons of mass destruction (WMD). The occupation of Kuwait had economic motives, as a way of solving the challenge of indebtedness, but the urgency came because indebtedness was aggravating Saddam's overall strategic predicament.

Preoccupied by the excitement and demands of the end of the Cold War, the NATO countries missed the development of this crisis. Even when Iraqi forces began to mobilize en masse close to the Kuwait border in late July, Washington was content to accept assurances from other Arab states that this was largely a bluff. As a result the crude and brazen Iraqi invasion of Kuwait came as more of a shock than it need have done and led to questions about whether inadvertently a "green light" had been given to Saddam. On the assumption that what was going on in the Gulf was a bit of political theater, that Saddam would not do anything so rash as to invade his neighbor, American policymakers had confined themselves to commenting on their limited security commitments to Kuwait and their desire to be friends with everyone, without ever reminding Iraq that a blatant disregard of the most basic international prohibition against aggression was bound to trigger some sort of response. If there had been a defense treaty with Kuwait (something which it along with the other Gulf States had hitherto been reluctant to contemplate) that might have helped deter Iraq. The issue became irrelevant after the invasion because the issue was now whether the international community could rise to the challenge of aggression.

Two factors ensured a quick response. First was the failure of Iraqi forces to capture the Emir and other key members of the al-Sabah family before they escaped to Saudi Arabia. If they had been able coerce the Royal Family into accepting a new status under Iraqi "protection," then the international response might have been more muted. Second was recognition that the Iraqis would try to gain access to Kuwait's wealth, which required urgent action, especially from Washington and London, to freeze Kuwaiti assets held by overseas banks. Both factors made it possible for the Security Council to consider the invasion as a breach of the peace under Chapter VII of the UN Charter, thereby making possible tough action "to restore international peace and security."

In this way the crisis made the transition from the strategic perspectives of the Cold War era even sharper than it might otherwise have been. Instead of the traditional preoccupation with the integrity of alliances, the discourse switched naturally and immediately to one of maintaining the norms of international order—from realism to idealism in the blink of an eye.

The change can be illustrated by considering the response, or more accurately the lack of response, in the United Nations when Iraq had last engaged in aggression by invading Iran almost exactly a decade earlier. In contrast to 1990 when there was a determined

Security Council response to Iraqi aggression, the refusal to take a stand in 1980 was considered shameful at the time. Then the two superpowers were going through a tense phase, described as the "second Cold War," to distinguish it from the détente of the early 1970s. By 1990 relations between Washington and Moscow were close and cooperative as they worked together on winding down the Cold War. Their ability to consult and reach common positions became progressively more important during the course of the conflict.

Yet though this represented a momentous transformation in international affairs by itself it does not explain what had changed since 1980. The United States and the Soviet Union had not lined up on opposing sides in the Iraq-Iran war. Because of the Iranian revolution of January 1979, and the subsequent seizure of US diplomatic hostages, relations between Tehran and Washington had moved with startling speed from warm to hostile. This appeared to give Moscow an opportunity to engineer yet another dramatic shift in local alignments. It implied that it would abandon its Iraqi client as warm messages were sent to Iran, even finding a role for religious fundamentalism in Marxist doctrine. But the clerics in Tehran were not about to embrace an atheistic communist state that was engaged in an anti-Muslim campaign in Afghanistan. So despite being the victim, Iran was friendless.

Meanwhile Iraq was able to broaden its international support, beyond its established relations with the Soviet Union and France, by playing on anxieties about Iranian intentions and in particular the fear of a new Persian crusade. During the course of the 1980s Baghdad developed trade with western countries, including the United States, which extended, largely through the acquisition of dual-use technologies, into the military sphere. These relations were barely affected by Iraq's use of chemical weapons against Iran and its own people. The prevailing view up to the crisis was realist,

in its most cynical form. The argument was that it was worth per-
severing with Saddam, despite his indebtedness, bombastic rhetoric, and evident preoccupation with military strength, including
weapons of mass destruction, for reasons of trade and a lingering
hope that his pragmatism might lead him into moderation.

By 1990 however this was wearing thin. The ties had become
attenuated and were insufficient to cause either Washington or
Moscow a moment's hesitation once the invasion occurred. In
Russia there was more residual support for Iraq, but this tended
to be among the old communist hard-liners whose position had
become more marginal over the late 1980s. By contrast Kuwait in
1990 was much closer to the West than Iraq and certainly more so
than Iran in 1980. Even without a direct defense relationship, the
United States had spent the previous few years protecting Kuwaiti
oil tankers (ironically because of Kuwait's support for Iraq in the
war with Iran). Kuwait had also, unusually for a Gulf State, reasonable relations with the Soviet Union.

The main geostrategic difference between 1980 and 1990,
however, lay in the attitudes of other Arab governments. In 1980
(with the exception of Syria) they had warned western countries
against criticizing Iraq, arguing successfully that its actions should
be understood as a reasonable response to the deeply subversive
behavior of the new Iranian government. In 1990 Arab governments felt that they had been misled by Saddam about his intentions. The Saudis understood that whether or not, as the Americans
were suggesting, they were next in line for a military invasion,
if Iraq were able to get away with occupying and then annexing
Kuwait, the resultant shift in the local balance of power would
have left them at a particular disadvantage. The Saudi reaction was
critical. It set the terms for other Arab countries, with Syria in this
case working with the mainstream. It also meant that not only was

their support for immediate economic sanctions, but these could be enforced and also the wherewithal was soon in place for military action.

One lesson to be drawn from this episode was that expeditionary military interventions by western countries are very dependent on regional attitudes, for both diplomatic and logistical reasons. If the Saudis had decided that the Kuwaitis deserved their fate and that some modus vivendi could be found with the new Iraq/Kuwait combine, then there would not have been a lot that the United States could have done. If the Saudis had not accepted US forces on their territory, one of the most fateful decisions taken by Riyadh in recent decades, then the liberation of Kuwait by means of armed force would not have been possible. Here is a counterfactual to ponder. We might assume that some negotiated settlement would have allowed the Emir to return to a plundered Kuwait, and that Saddam would have continued to exert his influence as a strong and potentially disruptive international player. This might have provided a reason for the Iranians to return to closer ties with the West, while Osama bin Laden would have been denied his reason to rebel against his own country and take up arms against the United States for defiling by its presence in Saudi Arabia the sacred land of Mecca and Medina. As it was, the relevance of the crisis in terms of terrorism was whether Iraq's old friends among the more extreme Palestinian factions might mount some attacks on its behalf. Another hypothetical course for the conflict was a protracted, tense stand-off between Iraq and the rest of the international community in which the question of Iraqi WMD loomed larger and larger. If Saddam had waited until he could make a credible claim to a nuclear capability, then there is a further question about whether this would have counted as sufficient deterrent to encourage a much more cautious response from the United States and its allies.

These and other various alternative outcomes were considered early on in the crisis, as it was far from obvious during the critical first days following Iraq's invasion that Washington was interested in leading an international response, nor that Kuwait's neighbors—and in particular Saudi Arabia—believed western aid necessary or desirable. At first, the coalition military moves were presented as being precautionary and defensive. It was well into October before the possibility of offensive action, designed to eject Iraqi forces from Kuwait rather than just blunt their further aggression, began to be seriously considered. Up to that point, this was seen as a test case for coercive economic sanctions. This test was abandoned not because of doubts about how well sanctions might work, or Iraq's use of hostages as a form of counter-coercion, but because of the speed with which Kuwaiti infrastructure and society was being dismantled by the Iraqi occupation.

Where the new US-Soviet relationship was crucial was in sustaining a forceful stance having agreed that the Iraqi action constituted unacceptable aggression. Once the Security Council had recognized Kuwait's grievance and established a sanctions regime under Chapter VII, there was no need for constant referral back to the Council. Further measures, including military action, could have been undertaken under Article 51 of the Charter, which recognizes the inherent right to self-defense. Margaret Thatcher, the British Prime Minister for the first months of the crisis (she was deposed in an internal party coup in November 1990), had found Article 51 more than sufficient during the Falklands conflict of 1982 and recommended that Bush rely upon it as questions of force arose. These questions first arose in the context of enforcing sanctions by intercepting Iraqi ships. Bush, however, saw the opportunity to maintain a broad consensus of international support by working through the Security Council.[2] This would also help when it came to putting the issue to Congress. The key to this approach was making sure that Mikhail Gorbachev was supportive at each stage. This meant allowing him to use his remaining lines of communication with Baghdad to try to persuade Saddam to back down prior to each escalation. Initially it was supposed, not always enthusiastically, that Moscow and Baghdad might come to some arrangement. Eventually the conversations came to have a more ritualistic quality, although those that took place right at the end, in the days before the land war risked becoming part of Saddam's delaying tactics. So although the key commitments that led to the liberation of Kuwait were made as an almost reflex action to the Iraqi invasion, with economic sanctions appearing as an easy option, once the commitment had been made and Saddam had not backed down, it was the US-Soviet partnership that sustained the international consensus. This was hardly a partnership of equals: all the heavy lifting was done by the Americans. The Soviet contribution was not to cause difficulties.

III

It was also the US-Soviet partnership that gave Bush his notion of the potential implications of the management of this crisis for long-term international policy. Initially the President's line was that Iraqi aggression had jeopardized the hopes generated by the end of the Cold War. In early August 1990, he spoke of how without a response a "new era," which was "full of promise, an age of freedom, a time of peace for all peoples" would be put at risk. It took until September 11, 1990, before he set out the potential longer term implications of the conflict in an address to Congress. In this speech "a New World Order" was set as the fifth objective of

American policy (after immediate and unconditional Iraqi withdrawal from Kuwait, restoration of Kuwait's legitimate government, assurance of security and stability in the Gulf, and protection of American citizens). He spoke of a "unique and extraordinary moment" that offered a "rare opportunity to move toward an historic period of co-operation." He described the New World Order as a new era that would be:

> freer from the threat of terror, stronger in the pursuit of justice, and more secure in the quest for peace. An era in which the nations of the world, East and West, North and South, can prosper and live in harmony.[3]

After Desert Storm, Bush sought to spell out the implications of this New World Order. He offered the following definition:

> The New World Order does not mean surrendering our national sovereignty or forfeiting our interests. It really describes a responsibility imposed by our successes. It refers to new ways of working with other nations to deter aggression and to achieve stability, to achieve prosperity and, above all, to achieve peace. It springs from hopes for a world based on a shared commitment among nations large and small to a set of principles that undergird our relations—peaceful settlement of disputes, solidarity against aggression, reduced and controlled arsenals, and just treatment of all peoples.

The vision, despite the use of the word "new" was actually conservative. The new world was rather similar to the old except that it would lack some of its less agreeable features. What was important was that in this case a regional conflict had not served as a proxy for superpower confrontation; the United Nations Security Council functioned as intended as nations from all around the world joined together against an aggressor. There was no promise of "an era of perpetual peace" but more a way of keeping the "dangers of disorder at bay."[4] In effect this meant that that the international community was now better able to cope with challenges to its basic norms.

The management of the conflict saw what was in effect the Old World Order operating according to the hopes of those who wrote the charter of the United Nations during the closing months of World War II. The Permanent Five worked together in the Security Council to deplore Iraqi behavior and then work through the options allowed under Chapter VII to reverse the original aggression. The terms of international law were respected and military action was limited to what was necessary to deal with the matter at hand, and no more. The United States accepted limited objectives, based on the status quo ante bellum. The aim was very clearly the liberation of Kuwait and not of Iraq. In SC Resolution 687, terms were set for the cease-fire that allowed Saddam Hussein's regime to stay in power but also set stringent requirements for disarmament and general international behavior. This did not mean tolerating the continuation of Saddam Hussein's rule, but it did mean depending on Iraqis to bring it to a conclusion. Even when there was an insurrection as Desert Storm came to a conclusion, the United States held back.

Furthermore, by putting every move through the Security Council and putting together the broadest possible coalition, involving both familiar allies, in Britain and France, and Arabs, with the Saudis, Egyptians, and Syrians, the United States sought to avoid an over prominent position. When Bush and his advisors were concerned that the battering of retreating Iraqi forces was giving the impression of bullying, they called for a cease-fire. Everything was done to demonstrate that the United States was capable of sticking to the terms of UN resolutions and avoiding the acquisition of new missions during the course of the campaign. All this fitted in with the generally cautious approach of Bush's team that was evident throughout his Presidency.

There was a further tension between working within the United Nations and acting only according to the highest political standards. Multilateral diplomacy and fighting "coalitions of the willing" require compromises. As China, for example, was in a position to veto Security Council resolutions, it could use the crisis as an opportunity to end its post–Tiananmen Square isolation. Syria had been subject to recent condemnation for state terrorism but was now valued as a member of the anti-Iraq coalition who could represent the more radical Arab states. Iran remained a country with whom relations were poor but had to be persuaded against any temptation to form some alliance of convenience with its erstwhile Iraqi enemy. Members of the coalition—including Kuwait and Saudi Arabia—had poor human-rights records. The stand taken was essentially principled in terms of its opposition to aggression, and it was only the unambiguous and vicious nature of the aggression that made it possible to forge such a coalition, this was a coalition with a common cause that could not go much further than the rights of states.

This was one reason to be cautious about a potential alternative and more radical interpretation of the New World Order that picked up on the ambition of the goals. Experience warned against taking these descriptions of a better world too seriously. The desiderata listed were standard fare for speeches of this sort. Who could be against peaceful dispute settlement, opposition to aggression, arms control and disarmament, and just treatment for all? The idea that if the major powers could consult and cooperate then the problems of the world could be managed satisfactorily and without major upset depended on ignoring issues of humanitarianism and justice and concentrating on security. The idealistic Wilsonian strand, which is always present in American policymaking, was at low ebb in the Bush Administration. Its mainstream realist approach meant that, in strategic if not always human terms, invading another country mattered more than oppressing one's own people.

IV

The upheavals of the early 1990s encouraged the view that however dangerous in principle the Cold War might have been, in practice it had given structure and stability to international politics. From this perspective, the most urgent requirement was to provide something comparable for whatever was going to follow. The most important aspect of President Bush's outline of the New World Order was not so much its goals as the fact that its character would be defined by the United States. It was best placed to decide what counted as an issue to be addressed by the international community. The commentator Flora Lewis noted that the rules of international behavior Bush had in mind might be needed, but this did not constitute a new world order—just a more orderly world. A call from Washington for order "chills practically everyone else," because it sounded suspiciously like a *Pax Americana*.[5]

Unavoidably, the New World Order's essential feature was less the values it was supposed to embody, or the principles which would shape its management, but that the United States would be at its center. The Bush Administration's ambitions may have been modest and conservative, with little interest in meddling in local affairs around the globe, but with a position clearly at the top of the international hierarchy should it opt for a much greater ambition then it was not clear how it could be stopped. This was reinforced by its economic and diplomatic strength. During the course of the negotiation of Resolution 678, which authorized the use of "all necessary means" to get Iraq out of Kuwait, Secretary of State James Baker was observed engaging in unequivocal arm-twisting to ensure that the resolution was passed overwhelmingly. There was soon talk of "a unipolar moment." In the Pentagon there was consideration of how to maintain the predominance that the United States now enjoyed as an objective in itself. Whatever the language in which it was couched, the core issue was one of American power.

This was something of a turnaround. Only a couple of years earlier the talk had been of American decline as a result of imperial overstretch. The Americans, it was argued, had been trying to do too much and risked going the way of past great powers, while the more nimble Asian producers, such as Japan and South Korea, forged ahead economically. Even in 1990-91, the US economy was not in great shape and arguably some of the most serious risks accepted were economic as much as military. If the rise in the price of oil occasioned by the crisis had persisted, then this could have aggravated the recession. In the event low oil prices followed the successful conclusion of the war. If the war had gone badly, it could have undermined American economic, as well as military, confidence.

Prior to Desert Storm the doubts had also extended to the military prowess of the United States. In 1990 there were still many doubts about the competence of the armed forces. One of the achievements of Desert Storm according to the President was that the United States had got over "the Vietnam Syndrome" by which he meant that the United States had shown that it was prepared to use force and prevail, even at risk of casualties. Certainly there had been a lot of loose talk about how the Americans would give up as soon "as the body bags come home." There were also regular claims, which turned out to be poorly founded, that there would be serious losses among coalition forces. The growing qualitative strength of the US armed forces, at least when it came to regular warfare, had been obscured by previous encounters involving either jungles or cities, and in such politically complex situations such as Vietnam or Lebanon. Victories in Grenada (1980) and Panama (1989) or the bombing of Tripoli (1986) did not really count because of the weak nature of the opposition. Even then, there were elements of incompetence in the American performance, which led to the argument that a focus on the procurement of major weapons systems had diminished the ability to grasp the fundamentals of the military art. When it came to Desert Storm, the United States took seriously its military preparations, amassing a large force and a plan that any suggestion of a muscle-bound and bumbling military was eradicated. The image of American power was enhanced and reinforced.

This sweeping victory undermined any notion that "Third World" countries could compete with the West in the military sphere, at least when fighting a regular war. Whatever arms acquired from western states, sophisticated intelligence, command and control, and training was still lacking. There was no question that the United States was in a different military class because of the sheer size and range of its military establishment. It was hard to imagine any government picking over the details of the Gulf War and working out how the United States could be defeated in a regular war. The logical response was to prepare for irregular war, and by the end of the 1990s that response was well understood, and during the 2000s the harsh reality of irregular war had to be confronted in Afghanistan and in Iraq again.

V

The reference to "just treatment for all" in Bush's presentation of the New World Order might, with the benefit of hindsight, seem to presage the humanitarian intervention of the 1990s. Up to this point the rights of states (noninterference in internal affairs) had taken priority over those of individuals and minority groups. After this point the balance shifted, with the action on behalf of the Kurds just after the war taken as the start of the trend. Not too much should be made of this. Issues of justice would regularly make appearance in lists of this sort, if only to avoid an illiberal and state-oriented impression, without being intended to be taken too seriously. In practice the issue was complex and controversial, raising issues of sovereignty, double standards, and unintended consequences. Forms of injustice are many and various, and can be in tension with each other. Given the evident reluctance of this Bush Administration to engage in humanitarian intervention, it is therefore doubtful if this was being marked out as a likely feature of the New World Order. If that had been the intention, then this complex set of issues would have deserved much more than a throwaway line.

Yet a degree of foresight would have encouraged a sharper focus on this issue. It was already apparent that it was going to become more contentious as "realist" strategic reasons for ignoring the internal behavior of repressive states subsided, and as the internal affairs of many members of the former Soviet bloc showed symptoms of violence and tension. The issue came up in an awkward and conspicuous fashion in the form of the postwar insurrection in Iraq. Although Bush went out of his way to insist that the United States would not get involved in an Iraqi civil war[6] (the experience of getting caught up in the Lebanese civil war in 1982-83 were still fresh, along with those of Vietnam), it turned out to be difficult to stand aside. As Saddam's forces pushed desperate Kurds to flee toward Turkey, only for them to be blocked and trapped at the border, passivity appeared as insensitive. The media were still in the region in numbers, reporting back on the plight of the Kurds, and there were reminders of Bush apparently encouraging them to rebel during the later stages of Desert Storm.

Unusually the European response to the developing tragedy was quicker than the American. From France and Britain came proposals for safe havens for the Kurds, within northern Iraq, and the Americans felt they could not block action. In terms of its objectives, which was to stop Kurds from fleeing into Turkey by enabling them to live more or less safely in northern Iraq, the safe havens policy was successful. But it also drew the Americans into Iraq's internal politics. Although it was possible to reduce the level of commitment, relying on a "no-fly zone" rather than troops on the ground, so long as Saddam remained in power the issue could not be resolved. The initiative divided the international community: the Soviet Union and China both saw this intervention in domestic Iraqi matters as a potentially dangerous precedent, with their own Baltic and Tibetan situations in mind. Within months similar issues about whether outside powers can have a responsibility to prevent severe oppression and humanitarian catastrophes arose as Yugoslavia began its painful disintegration, with first Croatia and then Bosnia-Herzegovina pleading for help. The Bush Administration was clearly unenthusiastic about these cases as well, and left the Europeans to do what they could. So the United States was a reluctant intervener, and there is no reason to suppose that Bush was at all interested in turning the United States into a campaigner for a more just world. Nonetheless, the issue of how to respond to violent instability was now firmly on the agenda with a clear precedent. Safe havens for the Kurds began the series of humanitarian interventions that continued for the rest of the decade.

Up to this point the overall European contribution, with the exception of Britain and France, had been minimal. The drama of the crisis took over from integration of the previously divided continent. A unified Germany had looked like a potential power broker of the 1990s, but its constitutional and political inhibitions against acting in any mode other than its own self-defense meant that its shows of solidarity took the form of subventions to help pay the costs of those who could use armed force. In the post-Cold War euphoria the talk was of new forms of political association, coming together after decades of separation, managing conflicts without violence. The events in the Gulf could be presented as a throwback to an earlier, more brutish period in international affairs, while Europe prepared itself for a progressive process of economic and political union. Unfortunately, Europeans were more dependent on oil from the Gulf than the Americans, and their nationals were as likely to be taken as hostage by the Iraqis, at least during the first weeks of the conflict. In addition the Americans had adopted a meticulously multilateral approach, successfully invoking Chapter VII of the UN Charter, so it was impossible to stand aside. Japanese leaders demonstrated a similar ambivalence to the international effort, initially largely concerned about protecting trade. Europe was, however, in a different place, and so was caught out in the middle of optimistic thoughts about how its new circumstances could facilitate an exemplary and mature approach to crisis management. The humanitarian issues associated with the Safe Havens initiative were picked up first by Europeans but the initiative could not succeed until the Americans signed up. In both sets of conflicts, the British and French tended to act more in their roles as Permanent Members of the Security Council than members of the European Community (soon to be Union). The prospective pooling of the power of a whole continent had created an expectation that an incisive and capable European Union could be one of the more striking features of the New World Order. The Gulf War might have been dismissed as the wrong sort of test, coming too soon, inadequate for a proper evaluation of European claims. Unfortunately, the limits of the European Union in terms of collective decision making and capacity were subsequently confirmed in the floundering over the breakup of Yugoslavia, a crisis in the neighborhood and one that European leaders claimed to be uniquely suited to the Community's capabilities and responsibilities.

VI

The paradox in the war's outcome lay in the gap between what might have been achieved if the coalition had employed its superior power to the full and what was actually achieved. The determination to show restraint, to fight conspicuously to the letter of the UN resolutions, avoiding mission creep, meant that the outcome was something of a letdown. The fact that Saddam survived and was able to proclaim his survival as an Iraqi victory was irritating at the time and became even more so as he was able to ride out the March insurrection and later the various plots to overthrow his regime. It did not feel like a victory. It was not decisive in the traditional sense, in that the Iraqi army was not eliminated and the Iraqi state was not left defenseless. If the war had turned out to be the stiff fight anticipated by many commentators, then this restraint would have seemed prudent, a matching of ambition to capability. In the event, however, the abrupt conclusion of the war suggested faint-heartedness. There were perfectly good arguments to explain the reluctance to march on Baghdad, reflecting a desire not to have to take responsibility for running the country and to avoid provoking Iraq's partition and intervention by its neighbors. The result, however, was to leave residual uncertainty about the meaning of American power and the ruthlessness of its deployment.

The uncertainty continued. The Bush Administration put a lot of effort into trying to move forward on an Arab-Israeli peace process, taking advantage of Palestinian discomfiture at having become so closely tied to Saddam during the crisis, while challenging the Israeli government on its settlements policy. The Madrid Conference suggested that this was bearing fruit, but there was no real opportunity to follow up. In the run up to the 1992 presidential election George Bush was clearly vulnerable to the charge that he was too engrossed in foreign policy and insufficiently focused on the economy, and when James Baker was pulled out of the State Department to manage the re-election campaign the energy went out of American diplomacy. With Bush defeated, President Clinton focused as promised on domestic and economic issues, and at least in his first two years, appeared as cautious and if anything more confused by unfolding international events as his predecessor.

The United States undoubtedly emerged from the Persian Gulf War in a leading position, but with attention turning to domestic issues, it appeared disinclined to lead. In the Middle East, the Palestinians and the Israelis managed to take their own initiative rather than wait for Clinton to come up with one of his own. He sought to contain Iran, as well as Iraq, without seeking a decisive resolution of the conflict with either. The rise of al Qaeda was observed, but its seriousness was not fully appreciated. Retreats in Somalia and caution in Rwanda, Bosnia, and Haiti indicated a risk-averse administration. Washington appeared semi-detached as Europe struggled to cope with the traumas resulting from communism's collapse, although American interventions when they came, as with the decision to open up NATO membership to former Warsaw Pact countries and the operation in both Bosnia and Kosovo, were often decisive. In the Middle East it never quite used its full power to make the most of the opportunities for an Arab-Israeli peace or to deal with radical Islamism. If the American position overall strengthened during the 1990s, it was more as a result of the renewed dynamism of the economy.

Meanwhile, while relations within the Security Council never reverted back to Cold War levels of distrust, tensions grew. Russia, as the successor to the USSR, showed increasing signs of insecurity and irritation with NATO's expansion. By the start of the 2000s the good relations of a decade earlier had frayed. Russia and China had broken with the West over Kosovo, which in the end was handled outside of the UN system, while France had joined them over Iraq. When the new George W. Bush Administration entered office it apparently, or at least publicly, aspired to an even more limited international role. This was the point at which the events set in motion by the various upheavals of 1989-91—in Afghanistan, Pakistan, Chechnya, Bosnia, Kosovo, and Iran, as well as Iraq and Israel—began to come together in ways with which the "New World Order" could barely cope.

In principle, the makings of a New World Order were in place, if not necessarily in the grand and elevated form implied in some

American rhetoric. It had two critical features: the pre-eminent position of the United States and its allies within the international system; and, second, a series of precedents created during the Gulf crisis for collective international action against flagrant violations of international law. Of these the most clear-cut was the decisive response to aggression and the most uncertain was the response to the distress of the Kurds. The unequivocal nature of Iraqi aggression meant that in this respect the precedent was celebrated but the case was unlikely to be repeated. By contrast, the humanitarian issues exemplified by the Kurdish case meant that in this case the precedent was played down but it was in fact much more pertinent and soon new examples were soon coming thick and fast.

The description of a New World Order reflected an aspiration to manage a period of major upheaval with the institutional structures and power configurations developed over the previous forty-five years. In the event international affairs were overwhelmed and reshaped by the unruly economic and political forces that were already well in motion as a result of decolonization and which were aggravated by the end of the Cold War and also, eventually, the Gulf War.

[4]

THE LAST WAR SYNDROME: HOW THE UNITED STATES AND IRAQ LEARNED THE WRONG LESSONS FROM DESERT STORM

Michael R. Gordon

The American-led occupation of Iraq was fraught with so much difficulty that it is tempting to look at the 1991 Persian Gulf campaign as a textbook example of how to wage war.

In many ways, the Desert Storm campaign President George H. W. Bush initiated to evict Iraqi forces from Kuwait was everything the 2003 invasion was not. For the 1991 conflict, the United States deployed an overwhelming force, secured the backing of the United Nations, established limited objectives, ensured that much of the expense was assumed by allied nations, and quickly brought the fighting to a close. Contrast that with the under-resourced and extraordinarily ambitious exercise to carry out regime change and build democracy in Iraq, which was more prolonged and costly in terms of lives and treasure than even its fiercest champions anticipated.

Yet it is important to have a sober—and not idealized—understanding of the 1991 conflict in the Gulf to understand its implications for American military strategy and its consequences for the Middle East. The release of declassified American documents and captured memoranda from Saddam Hussein's archives has added to the store of material on each side's calculations and miscalculations and enabled historians to refine their assessments. Strikingly, it is clear that the Iraqi and American leadership drew some of the wrong lessons from Desert Storm and applied them in their rematch in 2003 with adverse consequences for each side.

As for the 1991 war, much was done right. President Bush's decision to use force to reverse Iraq's seizure of Kuwait was courageous and far less popular at home than many politicians prefer to remember. (The Senate resolution authorizing the use of force passed by a vote of 52 to 47.) The most politically expedient approach would have been to rely on economic sanctions to punish Saddam, a course that would not have assured the departure of Iraqi forces from Kuwait but would have forgone the risks of military action. Leaving Saddam in control of Kuwait's oil fields, however, would have added to the regime's ability to finance its programs to develop chemical, biological, and even nuclear arms, and encouraged the Iraqi leader to pursue a more aggressive policy in the region.

The effort to build a multinational coalition was skillfully executed. Secretary of State James A. Baker III secured support—and even financial backing—in foreign capitals for military action. Although the American forces did most of the fighting, it was helpful militarily to have British and French allies, and it was useful politically to have a coalition that included Arab troops, even if Egyptian forces marched into Kuwait City only after US Marines, supported by the Army's Tiger Brigade, did the hard work of retaking it. The massive American air and ground forces that were deployed turned out to be much more than was required. But the time it took to dispatch such a large force gave diplomats a final chance to try to avert the war and ensured that there were virtually no military scenarios in which the American-led coalition would be shorthanded.

Once the war was underway, the prowess of the American military was impressive. The superior training of the American all-volunteer force coupled with advanced military technology enabled the United States to prevail with surprisingly modest casualties. Seizing command of the skies, the United States took the air war to Baghdad at the outset of the conflict, and the American-led coalition prevailed in the land war that followed at a surprisingly modest cost to itself. The nearly 800,000-strong coalition lost 240 personnel in the fighting. Some 540,000 personnel were American and 148 of these were killed in action or died of their wounds.[1] Significantly, the dominance of American forces on the battlefield enabled the United States to overcome the Vietnam Syndrome, the immobilizing fear that the commitment of ground troops would ensnare the military in a bloody quagmire.

For all that, a close reading of each side's internal records, as well as interviews with key participants, points to a number of lapses and deficiencies. The Bush Administration systematically misread Saddam's intentions in the year leading up to his attack on Kuwait, as did virtually all of the Arab states and much of the international community. There were repeated indications that Saddam saw the presence of even modest American forces in the Middle East as an impediment to his designs in the region, as well as an instance in early 1990 in which a senior Iraqi official hinted that the regime coveted Kuwaiti territory.

Nor did the Bush Administration have an effective political and military strategy prior to Iraq's invasion to contain Iraqi power in the event that its diplomatic efforts to reach out to Saddam's regime fell short. Seeking to establish a dialogue with Saddam, the United States repeatedly sought to reassure the conspiracy-minded Iraqi leader that it harbored no ill intentions toward his regime, going so far as to promise him that it had no plans to carry out a preemptive strike on his then-active programs to develop weapons of mass destruction. The effort to try to moderate the behavior of the Iraqi leader was reasonable, but the failure to wield sticks, as well as carrots, left the United States unprepared after its efforts to engage Saddam failed.

Once the Desert Storm campaign was underway, efforts to bring the war to a close on terms most advantageous to the United States were hampered by the Bush Administration's desire for a swift military disengagement. Nor was the response to the ensuing upheaval in southern Iraq adequate, a rebellion the White House inadvertently encouraged by broadcasting appeals for the Iraqis to get rid of their leader, as even a leading member of Bush's inner circle now acknowledges.[2] As a result, the war was not as decisive as President Bush had hoped in undermining Saddam's grip on power and paving the way for a more stable Middle East. Saddam's overthrow went beyond the formal mandate of Desert Storm. Nonetheless, as the declassified accounts from the Bush presidential archives make clear, it was the President's firm hope that the war would facilitate the Iraqi dictator's exit—so much so that Bush repeatedly discussed the importance of ousting Saddam in confidential meetings with Middle East leaders before, during, and after the war.[3]

Indeed, the most enduring consequence of the 1991 conflict may be the way in which it laid the foundation for the harder war that was to follow. There was nothing inevitable about the American-led invasion of Iraq in 2003. The United States might have sought to reinforce its strategy to contain Iraq's presumed programs to develop chemical, biological, and nuclear arms, as well as the missiles to deliver them, by attempting to patch up a fraying sanctions regime rather than invading and taking on the monumental responsibilities of an occupying power. But the messy way in which the Gulf War was terminated contributed to the dilemma. Saddam's refusal to fully implement the disarmament obligations imposed by the United Nations after the 1991 conflict was at the core of the debate as to whether and how to use force in 2003 and provided the formal casus belli that the White House invoked for the American-led invasion.

Importantly, the Gulf War also shaped each side's military strategy for the rematch. Once the American invasion was underway, each side essentially refought the Desert Storm campaign. The United States anticipated in 2003 that its primary adversary would be Saddam's Republican Guard divisions, the most formidable force American troops had confronted in the Persian Gulf conflict a dozen years prior, and gave scant thought to the possibility that the greatest challenge would come from Sunni insurgents, Iranian-supported militias, and foreign fighters that would slip across a porous border. After toppling Saddam, it took almost four years for the United States to design and begin implementing a comprehensive counterinsurgency strategy.

As for Saddam, his main worry in 2003 was that the Shia and Kurds would rise up as they had at the end of the Gulf War. The United States had not ventured all the way to Baghdad in 1991 when they had a more substantial force in the region, and the Iraqi leader thought it unlikely before the 2003 war that American forces would take his capital. Indeed, Saddam's plans to put down a Shia rebellion, which included an edict not to destroy key bridges without the Iraqi leader's explicit authority so the spans could be used by Iraq's security forces, inadvertently abetted the American rush to Baghdad.

The result was an outcome for which neither side was prepared. Saddam, to his surprise, was chased from power but the Americans were confronted by a virulent insurgency that they had failed to anticipate and spent years trying to establish sufficient order in the country to facilitate its political development. There were numerous factors that contributed to the fraught situation— George W. Bush's disdain for nation building, Defense Secretary Donald Rumsfeld's pressure to carry out the invasion with the minimal force necessary, the ill-advised edicts by the Coalition Provisional Authority on de-Ba'athification and the dismissal of the Iraqi military and the Sunnis' reluctance to relinquish power to a Shia majority. But another factor was each side's proclivity to misread the lessons of the Gulf War.

|

In the two decades following Desert Storm, several new sources of documentation have become available. They include declassified transcripts of communications between President Bush and foreign leaders, as well as internal memoranda, which are housed at the George Bush Presidential Library and Museum at Texas A&M University.

Another source is an extraordinary Iraqi archive, which includes 2,300 hours of recorded meetings and millions of pages of documents, that was captured by US forces after the 2003 invasion. Some of this material has been cited in studies issued by the Joint Forces Command, and more than 27,000 pages have been declassified and made available at the National Defense University in Washington, DC, to scholars outside government.[4] Yet another source are the diplomatic cables from American embassies in the region made public by Wikileaks, which have been reported by the *New York Times*, the *Guardian*, and other publications. In conjunction with interviews with key participants, these records provide important details about American and Iraqi decision making and facilitate a deeper analysis of each side's strategies.

Even before President Bush took office in 1989 the United States sought to engage Saddam. Seeking to forestall an Iranian victory in the eight-year Iran-Iraq war, the Reagan Administration authorized the sharing of tactical intelligence with the Iraqi military. After Bush took office, he sought to improve ties with an Iraq that the United States hoped would serve as a bulwark against Iran's ambitions while encouraging Saddam to moderate his behavior. A classified Pentagon paper on "The Rise of Third World Threats" concluded that after its grueling war with Iran, Iraq would be "reluctant to engage in foreign military adventures."[5]

Despite the Bush Administration's efforts, however, Saddam remained wary of the United States' motivations. The Iran-Contra affair in which American arms were secretly shipped to Iran during the Reagan Administration prompted Iraqi complaints of American double-dealing.[6] Saddam was also unhappy with the United States' long-standing support for Israel. In an October 6, 1989, meeting with Secretary of State James A. Baker III, Iraqi Foreign Minister Tariq Aziz astounded the Americans by stating that Saddam had come to the conclusion that the United States was scheming to destabilize his government. The Iraqi leader feared that he might even be a target for assassination. Baker sent a cable that month instructing American diplomats in Baghdad to make clear that Washington did not harbor such a nefarious agenda.[7] Similar assurances were later personally conveyed to Saddam by Senator Robert Dole, who travelled to Iraq as part of a congressional delegation, he noted in an April 17, 1990, letter to Bush.[8]

None of that, however, seemed to satisfy Saddam, who appeared to see American forces as an impediment to his broader ambitions in the region. An early indication of Saddam's thinking was evident on February 16, 1990, when John Kelly, the Assistant Secretary of State for Near East and South Asian Affairs, met with the Iraqi leader in Baghdad. It was Kelly's first trip to the Gulf, and he was struck by Saddam's preoccupation with the Israeli-Palestinian dispute and his professed desire for strong relations with Washington. But Edward W. "Skip" Gnehm Jr., a deputy to Kelly, recalled that Saddam also sent a more disturbing message: the United States Fifth Fleet should be withdrawn from the Gulf.

"The way he did it was to muse," Gnehm recalled in an interview. "He started out by saying that the Iraq-Iran war was over and that there was really no threat at the moment. And then he kind of looked over our heads and says 'when I look southward in the Gulf what do I see? What is out there? A lot of ships? What kind of ships? Warships? And they are American warships. Why are American warships still in the Gulf when the war is over for all this time? Because of me? That can't be. I am not a threat. If so, they ought to take their ships and go home. They don't need to be there.'" Gnehm responded that the Fifth Fleet had been there since the final years of World War II and would, no doubt, be in the region long after Saddam and his guests were gone.[9]

That response did not sit well with Saddam, and a week later he went public with his complaints at the meeting of the Arab Cooperation Council in Jordan. Now that the Iran-Iraq war was over, Saddam said, it was time for the United States to withdraw its fleet. With the end of the Cold War and the retreat of Soviet power, Saddam continued, the United States might be the sole superpower. But even the mightiest nation had an "Achilles heel," he added, citing the withdrawal of American forces from Lebanon after the 1983 suicide attack on a Marine barracks in Beirut.[10] The Iraqi leader also called on Arab nations to use their oil reserves to create a counterweight to American power, comments that stirred concern at the highest levels of the State Department.

Iraq's frustrations with Kuwait also featured in another meeting that Kelly and Gnehm had in Baghdad. A senior Iraqi aide hosted the American diplomats at a dinner and pointedly asked why the Kuwaitis were holding onto the islands of Bubiyan and Warbah, which constricted Iraq's outlet to the Gulf. "We concluded that it was a message," said Gnehm. "They wanted us to know how important they saw these two islands to be and they were going to keep pursuing it. It did not necessarily mean force, but it troubled us that they brought it up the way that they did."[11]

Iraq had some history with Kuwait and it was not a happy one. Soon after Kuwait became independent in 1961, Abdul-Karim Qassim, Iraq's military strongman, claimed sovereignty over the neighboring Gulf State, arguing that it had originally been part of the Ottoman province of Basra. A portent of events to come, Qassim coveted Kuwait for its oil fields and coastline, an attractive asset for Iraq, whose only access to the sea was a naval base at Umm Qasr and the Shatt al-Arab, a waterway that was a regular source of contention between Iraq and Iran. Britain sent a brigade to Kuwait to deter an attack on its former protectorate, and the Kuwaitis sought to ease tensions by making substantial loans to Iraq, which were never repaid. Even during the Iran-Iraq war when Kuwait was helping to finance Saddam's military effort, an American intelligence officer who visited Iraq as part of the intelligence-sharing effort was struck by the disdain Iraqi officers expressed for the "bearded women" to their south.[12]

By April 1990, the deterioration in American-Iraqi relations had led the State Department to issue fresh instructions to April

Glaspie, the American ambassador in Baghdad. Saddam had taken some positive steps, the instructions noted, such as ending his attempts to intervene in Lebanon's tangled politics and agreeing to take part in a disarmament conference on chemical weapons. On the other side of the ledger, Saddam had criticized the American naval presence in the Gulf, Iraqi agents had been caught in a sting operation as they sought to smuggle nuclear warhead triggers from the United States and Iraq had also constructed Scud missile launchers in western Iraq that could reach Israel and American forces in southern Turkey. Glaspie was to raise these issues without unduly alarming the Iraqis. "As concerned as we are about Iraq's chemical, nuclear, and missile programs, we are not in any sense preparing the way for a preemptive military unilateral effort to eliminate these programs," the ambassador was instructed to add.[13]

By July, Iraq's policies on Kuwait had become a growing worry. Iraq was leveling complaints that Kuwait was surreptitiously drilling into Iraqi reserves, refusing to accept Iraq's delineation of the border, working to depress oil prices at a time when Iraq's economy was suffering and, in general, failing to recognize the sacrifices Iraq had made in fighting the Persians on behalf of the Arab world. Adding to the concern, Iraq did not demobilize large number of soldiers following the Iran-Iraq conflict. The Iraqi military was, in part, an employment program and there were not enough jobs in the civilian sector to absorb thousands of former soldiers. But the end result was that Iraq continued to have a massive army, one that did not fit with the earlier American assessments that Iraq was war-weary and disdainful of future military adventures.

On July 11, according to an intelligence report in the captured Iraqi archives, Iraq conducted a reconnaissance flight to identify targets in Kuwait.[14] The Iraqi document implies the aircraft flew over—and not merely near—Kuwaiti territory. Among the sites identified were oil facilities, military bases, radar sites, missile batteries, communications facilities, and broadcasting stations. It is not clear if the reconnaissance was detected by Kuwait or the United States. But Iraq's other military preparations later that month did not go unnoticed.

On July 16, Tariq Aziz, Iraq's foreign minister, sent a letter to the Arab league, charging that Kuwait's refusal to settle its border disputes with Iraq, its rejection of Iraq's demand that the multi-billion dollar debt it owed Kuwait be cancelled, and its alleged production of oil in excess of OPEC quotas amounted to military aggression. A week later, the British military attaché in Baghdad issued a report that made its way to the CIA: 3,000 vehicles, some from civilian ministries, had been seen heading toward the Kuwaiti border. Since the move was not visible to the Kuwaitis and was made at a time when the Iraqi economy could ill afford more disruption, it was seen by some at the CIA as a war preparation. Nobody could say if Saddam would pull the trigger, but intelligence analysts were persuaded he was creating a military option. On July 25, Charles Allen, the CIA's National Intelligence Officer for Warning, issued a "warning of war" asserting that there was a 60 percent chance that Iraqi forces would attack Kuwait.[15]

Iraqi bullying in the Gulf was not a new scenario for the Pentagon. A classified 1979 Pentagon study, which was drafted after Iraq sought to mobilize support against the Camp David accords ending the enmity between Egypt and Israel, noted the possibility of an Iraqi threat to the Arabian Peninsula. If the United States were to intervene, it should be "before hostilities began" at a time when "escalation might still be avoided," the study noted.[16] (The Pentagon officials who drafted the study included Dennis Ross, the future Middle East envoy, Paul Wolfowitz, who would rise to Deputy Defense Secretary during the presidency of George W. Bush and Geoffrey Kemp, who served as a Middle East expert on Ronald Reagan's National Security Council.)

As Iraq rattled the saber, planners at the US Central Command, which had responsibility for the Middle East region, drew up a list of additional military steps to signal Iraq not to attack and to modestly strengthen the US military posture in the region if he did. They included accelerating the deployment of an aircraft carrier to the North Arabian Sea, moving Maritime Prepositioning Ships filled with tanks and other military equipment to Saudi Arabia, sending a squadron of F-15s to the region, and dispatching B-52 bombers to Diego Garcia.

None of these precautionary moves were taken. The Bush Administration was reluctant to take steps that might be viewed as unduly provocative. Most Arab states in the Persian Gulf preferred to keep the American military over the horizon, and many American policymakers persuaded themselves that the Iraqis were merely posturing for effect. As tensions in the region grew, the United Arab Emirates asked the United States to send two KC-135 refueling tankers to extend the range of their French-made Mirage aircraft, a deployment that was carried out as part of an exercise dubbed "Ivory Justice." During the Iran-Iraq war, Iraqi planes had struck an offshore oil platform that belonged to the Emirates, and though the Iraqis had insisted the bombing was a mistake the Emirates was not so certain. Saudi Arabia and Egypt complained about the move, saying that the dispute between Iraq and Kuwait could be handled within the Arab family.[17]

While some of the United States' Arab allies in the Gulf viewed the modest step as an overreaction, it did not escape Iraq's notice. On July 25, Glaspie was called to a meeting with Saddam. The Iraqi leader recited a list of grievances against the Kuwaitis and spoke about the "blows" that relations between the United States and Iraq had suffered, including the Iraqi suspicion that the United States would have preferred that the Iran-Iraq war drag on forever and the American desire to see a reduction in the price of oil. The "maneuvers" the United States was conducting, Saddam added, referring to "Ivory Justice," would merely encourage Kuwaiti intransigence. During the meeting, Saddam stopped to take a phone call from Egyptian President Hosni Mubarak, who was helping to broker a round of negotiations in Jeddah between the Iraqis and Kuwaitis. Saddam said that he would take no action before the meeting and nothing afterwards if the Kuwaitis "give us some hope." Glaspie cabled an account of the meeting with the title: "Saddam's Message of Friendship to President Bush." The refueling exercise had gotten Saddam's attention and he was interested in a peaceful outcome, wrote Glaspie, who soon left Baghdad for a leave.[18]

The meeting, however, also allowed for another interpretation. During his meeting with Glaspie, Saddam had also offered the view that the United States, haunted by Vietnam Syndrome, could not endure casualties like a battle-hardened nation like Iraq—the same message he had delivered in his defiant February address in Jordan. Iraq, it seemed, wanted correct relations with Washington but on its own terms and was cautioning the United States about the risks of challenging Iraq's ambitions in the Gulf region.

At the White House and the State Department, the dominant view was that the crisis had passed. Ignoring Pentagon officials who favored a tougher message, the State Department instructed Glaspie on July 28 to welcome Iraq's interest in a negotiated solution and to add that a more comprehensive presidential message would be coming. But Iraq's military preparations continued. Satellite imagery showed that eight of Saddam's Republican

Guard divisions, some 120,000 troops and 1,000 tanks, had taken up positions just north of the Kuwaiti border, along with Iraqi Special Forces.

On August 1, Allen issued a "warning of attack," raising the possibility of an Iraqi move on Kuwait to 70 percent. Allen's classified memo noted that Saddam Hussein's objectives might include seizing Kuwait City and deposing the Kuwaiti ruling family, a possibility dismissed by some more senior intelligence officers who thought it more likely that any Iraqi aggression would be limited to the seizure of Failaka and Bubiyan islands. Then Allen headed to the White House to personally deliver the warning to Richard Haass, the senior director on the NSC for Near East and South Asia Affairs. Similar warnings were issued by the Defense Intelligence Agency.[19]

It was not the most auspicious time for the crisis. Bush had been preparing to deliver a major speech explaining his decision to make a series of defense cuts, which critics of the Pentagon had been clamoring for after the end of the Cold War.[20] Despite the warning from Allen, Bush Administration officials spent much of the day debating what Saddam was up to before concluding that the President should try to call Saddam to make an eleventh hour appeal to forestall a possible attack. As the President and his advisers were discussing how best to reach Saddam in the middle of the night, the American embassy in Kuwait City reported that Iraq had already invaded.[21]

The next day American diplomats in Baghdad contacted the Iraqi Foreign Ministry but received the brush off from Nizar Hamdun, a senior Iraqi official. "We have tried repeatedly since 0630 local to reach senior MFA officials," reported Joseph Wilson, the Deputy Chief of Mission. "Undersecretary Hamdun is apparently not at home since nobody answers his home telephone number. The Foreign Ministry duty officer is aware of our interest in talking to the minister, and we are reminding them every ten minutes. At 0710 local we were told that both Hamdun and the Foreign Minister were in a meeting."[22] Eventually, Wilson was provided with a prepared statement asserting that the episode was an internal affair for the new Kuwaiti authorities, the ones that would presumably be installed by Iraq. Mubarak later complained that Saddam had been duplicitous by promising not to take military action before he pursued negotiations with the Kuwaitis. But Iraq's archives show that Saddam had a very literal view of his assurance. According to the state-controlled media, Saddam had merely promised not to strike until the negotiations in Jeddah began.[23]

The Iraqi military's ability to achieve surprise put the United States at a huge disadvantage. The American and allied buildup that would be organized to defend neighboring Saudi Arabia would need to start virtually from scratch and under the wary eyes of the Iraqi occupiers. And instead of dissuading an Iraqi attack on Kuwait, American forces would need to roust the Iraqi troops from their newly fortified positions there. Even for a superpower it was an unenviable situation.

There was a larger lesson to be learned by American officials about the dangers of letting policy assumptions and the views of allies color their reading of the facts. Unlike other attacks that caught the United States unprepared, the Iraqi invasion of Kuwait did not stem from an intelligence community failure. Leading analysts at the CIA and DIA had repeatedly warned of Iraq's military buildup on Kuwait's doorstep. Intelligence analysts like Allen saw the Iraqi logistical preparations for what they were. It was the policy experts at the NSC and State Department who—influenced by the views of the Egyptians, the Saudis, and the Kuwaitis themselves— were inclined to the interpretation that the war preparations were no more than a bluff. After Iraq seized Kuwait the campaign to reverse that aggression was described as a "war of necessity."[24] Following Saddam's invasion of Kuwait, evicting the Iraqi forces there was indeed a strategic imperative. But it was still a war that did not necessarily need to happen. A red line was drawn but only after Saddam had crossed it.

II

Once it became clear that the United States was prepared to reverse the Iraqi invasion by force, it was Saddam's regime that was guilty of the most egregious miscalculations. Iraq's military strategy was an embodiment of the adage that when generals do not know what to do, they do what they know. Iraq had emerged from the Iran-Iraq war with a million-strong military equipped with Soviet tanks and French- and Soviet-made aircraft, including some capable of mid-air refueling. It had towed and self-propelled artillery from South Africa, Austria, and France and enough heavy trucks to transport an armored corps. It also had Scud missiles and a sizable arsenal of chemical weapons.

Still, Iraq had no experience fighting a superpower with precision firepower, stealth technology, modern command and control, and ground units trained in maneuver warfare. The war with Iran had been a grinding war of attrition, and Saddam prepared for more of the same. Tightening their grip on Kuwait, Iraqi forces established a defense-in-depth. The least capable and most expendable forces were arrayed just north of the Kuwaiti border with Saudi Arabia along what came to be known as the Saddam Line, a fortified frontier replete with mine belts, sand berms, bunker complexes, and ditches that could be filled with oil and set aflame. Fearful of an amphibious landing, the Iraqis also fortified Kuwait's coastline. Armored and mechanized units were arrayed in the interior of Kuwait, along with copious artillery. Behind this tier were the Republican Guards, the most loyal and formidable units in Saddam's army.[25]

Saddam's calculation was that any American or allied force that sought to liberate Kuwait would be weakened and bloodied as it bulled its way through Iraq's defensive barriers and was pummeled by artillery. When the location of the American attack was pinpointed, Iraq's mechanized reserves would rumble forward to halt the advance. Finally, Republican Guard armored and mechanized forces would race into battle and deliver the coup de grace. The nation that had been defeated in Vietnam would either shrink from the confrontation or find itself ensnared in a casualty-producing quagmire that would induce the American public to clamor for an end to the fighting.

For the Bush Administration, the first step was to ensure the defense of Saudi Arabia and its oil fields. But after that was accomplished the White House began to set its sights on the next phase: rolling back the Iraqi conquest. The goal was not just to evict Iraqi forces from Kuwait and restore the emir to power. Another important objective was to deprive Saddam of the offensive capability to again menace Kuwait and other Persian Gulf States. In a memo entitled "U.S. (Coalition) War Objectives and War Termination," Haass spelled out the goal, using the acronym for the Kuwaiti Theater of Operations. The aim was, Haass wrote:

> The physical destruction of enough of the Iraqi military machine to eliminate any significant offensive capability and the retention of sufficient military capability, to prevent Iraq from becoming a power vacuum (unable to deter or prevent

dismemberment by one of its neighbors.) These objectives could perhaps be best achieved by the destruction of Iraqi forces in the KTO—or their neutralization by removal of their tanks, artillery, armored personnel carriers.[26]

CENTCOM officials expressed the goal more bluntly: the goal was the destruction of Saddam's Republican Guard forces south of the Euphrates.[27]

In designing a campaign plan, the United States allotted air-power an enormous role. An elaborate plan was devised to destroy Iraq's air defense network so that allied airplanes could operate at high-altitude beyond the range of Iraq's abundant arsenal of anti-aircraft artillery. Iraqi targets would be pounded for weeks, including in Baghdad, whose command and communications facilities would be struck in the opening round, well before the ground war was underway. It was the fervent hope of American air war commanders that this alone would be sufficient to win the war. That would frustrate Saddam's plans to turn Kuwait into a meat grinder that American forces would have to traverse to dislodge their Iraqi adversaries.

If and when American and coalition ground forces were needed, the plan was for the Marines, fortified by an Army armored brigade, to attack into Kuwait and draw the attention of Iraqi commanders. The Army's VII Corps, buttressed by the British 1st Armored Division, which was deployed to the west of the Marines in Saudi Arabia, would cross into Iraq to outflank the Republican Guards. The Army's XVIII Airborne Corps, reinforced by the French, was deployed in far western desert in Saudi Arabia and would also participate in the envelopment.

Two weeks after the American-led air war began, Iraqi military leaders saw no sign of an allied ground attack. Saddam had not bargained on such an extended and one-sided air war. Improvised measures to protect Iraqi armor, such as surrounding tanks with a multitude of anti-aircraft weapons and sand berms, were of little value. American aircraft were able to pick out the tanks at night using their infrared target systems and destroy them with laser-guided bombs. Bit by bit, the sizable Iraqi force was being cut down to size and the morale of Iraqi forces was starting to plummet. Saddam concluded that if there was to be a casualty-inducing ground war Iraq would need to start it.

On January 27, 1991, Saddam went to Basra to discuss the plan with his field commanders: a two-division attack on Saudi Arabia supplemented by a commando raid at sea. It was not possible for the Iraqis to conceal all of their moves, but without a framework on the allied side for interpreting them they were seen as being of little consequence. Thanks to the American program of sharing intelligence during the Iran-Iraq war, Iraqi war planners also had some understanding of what the Americans could glean through overhead reconnaissance, which the Iraqis planned to exploit to achieve surprise. After the attack began, Lieutenant General Charles Horner, the air component commander, marshaled allied airpower and directed it against the Iraqi ground forces. The Iraqi seaborne attack was quickly squelched. But an Iraqi mechanized battalion managed to roar down the coastal highway and take the Saudi town of Khafji.[28]

Supported by a massive amount of American airpower, a Saudi-led force succeeded in retaking the town. The episode showed that the Iraqi army could not execute a multidivisional operation under the protection of obsolescent mobile anti-aircraft guns against a modern adversary rich in airpower. Although Schwarzkopf did not see the episode as of great military significance, it was one of the most important milestones in the war.

Convinced the Iraqis could be quickly defeated, Marine commanders overhauled their strategy for retaking Kuwait, opting for a speedier plan in which two Marine divisions would each breach the Iraqi fortifications.

As the ground war approached, the captured Iraqi archives reveal, Saddam began to appreciate his predicament and appealed to the Soviet Union to intercede. But with little understanding of the American-Soviet relationship, Saddam did not realize that Gorbachev and Bush were more interested in preserving their ties than saving Iraq's forces from the American-led juggernaut. Gorbachev did make an effort to delay the ground war and open the door to a negotiated pull-out of Iraqi forces, but the Soviet diplomacy was undermined when Saddam ordered Kuwaiti oil wells set ablaze, a move the Iraqi leader intended as a defensive tactic to foil allied reconnaissance and targeting. Bush denounced the move in his conversations with Gorbachev as a "scorched-earth policy" and a reason not to put off military action.[29] With little accurate intelligence, Mr. Hussein initially mistook some probing actions by the American military as signs that a major attack had been mounted and contained. "If this is the initial shock," Mr. Hussein said on the first day of the ground war, "then the attack has failed," according to an American translation of the Iraqi transcript of the meeting. In fact, Iraq's defensive strategy was undone.[30]

But the pounding the Iraqis had taken from the air and their failed Khafji operation had inadvertently created a major problem for the American strategy as well. The American-led strategy had been to use the Marine assault in Kuwait to draw in the Iraqis. Iraq's mechanized reserves and Republican Guard forces were to be focused on the American attack to their south when the Army's VII and XVIII Corps enveloped them from the west. The Iraqi troops were so weakened and battered, however, that the Marines sliced through them. Instead of luring the Iraqis into a kill zone the Marine attack acted like a piston pushing them out. The Iraqis began to flee, and the war quickly turned into a footrace.

Schwarzkopf was prepared for an array of problems: chemical weapons, fire trenches, and missile attacks. What he did not have was a plan to quickly exploit success. Under Schwarzkopf's plan, the Army VII Corps was to attack a day after the Marines, and the corps had difficulty accelerating its timetable.

The XVIII Airborne Corps, which began its operation on the day of the Marine offensive, did better. Led by Major General Barry McCaffrey, the Army's 24th Mechanized Division pressed the attack along the Euphrates headed toward Basra along with the 101st Airborne Division. An ardent advocate of the Army's helicopter assault capabilities, Major General Binford Peay, the commander of the 101st, made plans to airlift an entire brigade across the Euphrates by Chinook and Blackhawk helicopters and deploy it north of Basra. Three infantry brigades would block the Iraqi flight north protected by Apache helicopters and warplanes. Whoever slipped through the 24th Mech's grasp would be blocked by the 101st.

Lieutenant General Walter Boomer, who led the Marine attack, was also in a position to chase after the remnants of the Republican Guard. "Once we blew through with two divisions they were not going to be able to stop us," he said, referring to the Marine assault into Kuwait. "I think the speed surprised some, but it did not surprise us." Boomer informed Schwarzkopf by radio that he was already at Kuwait's border with Iraq. "I said, 'We are poised to launch to Basra and we will police up the rest of these folks if you want us to.' He said, 'Stand by.'"[31]

The enthusiasm for definitively shutting the door on the Iraqi army was shared by mid-level officials in the Pentagon. Arthur

Hughes, a deputy assistant Secretary of Defense for Near East and South Asia, drafted a memo that outlined a plan to reduce Iraq's military potential. The American army would seal off the Euphrates. Iraqi soldiers would have no choice but to leave their vehicles and walk north.

But as the war was raging other officials were less focused on the mission of eliminating Iraq's offensive military potential and began to weigh other factors. In Riyadh, Schwarzkopf broached the idea with his staff of having a five-day ground war, which he insisted would beat Israel's 1967 war with the Arabs by one day. (The Arab-Israel war had not been preceded by five weeks of bombing, but nobody made that point to the CENTCOM commander.) Schwarzkopf was not aware of Peay's plan to move a brigade north of Basra and said after the war that he would have opposed it had he known.

Enveloped in the fog of war Bush and his advisers were not focused on the flight of Iraq's Republican Guards but on the pummeling the Iraqis had taken as they fled Kuwait City. Iraqi forces had been caught on Mutla Ridge north of the Kuwaiti capital by American warplanes as they tried to escape north. No photos had yet appeared in the media, but when they did it would be a tableau of destruction. Eager to avoid a charge of piling on, as Defense Secretary Dick Cheney later put it, Bush and his war cabinet, with the strong encouragement of General Colin Powell, the chairman of the Joint Chiefs of Staff, decided to end the ground war at 100 hours. The United States' closest ally went along with the move. Douglas Hurd, the British Foreign Secretary, was in the Oval Office meeting where the decision was made. Margaret Thatcher, who had been so resolute in insisting that the Iraqi aggression be reversed, left office in November and her successor John Major lacked her tough-minded instincts. The British were prepared to defer to the Americans.

The decision to end the war was a judgment call. The move appeared more reasonable in Washington than in the field where commanders had a better sense that much of the Republican Guard was slipping away. Schwarzkopf was comfortable with the decision, but his deputy Lieutenant General Calvin Waller objected. After Waller learned of the deliberations in Washington, Waller uttered an expletive. "Then you go argue with them," Schwarzkopf replied.[32]

Barry McCaffrey, the major general who commanded the 24th Mech, was dumbfounded by the move. Boomer never heard back from Schwarzkopf on his offer to drive toward Basra. "The next message I received was not directly from him, but through my headquarters that we had in fact stopped," Boomer recalled. "I continue to be asked if we stopped too soon," Boomer added. "The answer in retrospect is 'Yes.'"[33]

Paul Kern, one of McCaffrey's brigade commanders who went on to rise to the rank of general, recalled, "There was a sense of success and a sense of concern at the same time. I knew that this would be a military decision that would be debated for years to come in terms of where we stopped. The sense was 'success, but ...'"[34]

According to intelligence data gathered soon after the cease-fire, a quarter of Iraq's tanks in the Kuwaiti theater (842 tanks in all) escaped as of March 1, 1990. Of these, 365 were T-72s, which meant that half of the Republican Guard's armor had gotten away.[35] Significantly, headquarters units also survived, which enabled the Iraqis to reconstitute the routed force that made it across the Euphrates and quickly put down the Shia uprising that arose in the south in the wake of the Iraqi defeat. Of the senior officers captured during the war, only one was a member of Republican Guard. Some additional Iraqi armor was destroyed by McCaffrey's division in the confusion that followed the cease-fire, but the larger point remains: in his triumphal news conference, Schwarzkopf boasted that the gate had been shut on the Iraqi forces in the Kuwaiti theater. In fact, the barn door was never closed and a lot of the horses got out.

In a telephone call on the last day of the ground war, Bush asked King Fahd bin Abdul Aziz Al Saud, the Saudi monarch: what were the chances of Saddam "being thrown out by his disillusioned people?" Fahd said that the Saudis were working with Iraqi exiles that had contacts inside of Iraq and were interested in getting rid of Saddam.

"If there is anything the United States can do to have him pushed out, I'd be very interested to hear it," Bush said. "We have no fight with the Iraqi people but I don't see how we can have improved, comfortable relations if he is in power."[36]

As the war drew to a close, some senior Bush Administration officials expected that Saddam would likely be overthrown within six months by Iraqis furious at a leader who had led them into two disastrous wars. During the lead-up to the war, Bush had suggested that the Iraqis take matters into their own hands and overthrow the Iraqi dictator, an appeal that was intended for the Iraqi military and other Ba'athists. Cheney was confident enough of that outcome that he placed a bet that Saddam would be gone a couple of years after the war ended.[37] But there was little reason to think that an authoritarian leader who ruled by fear would be so easily deposed.

Saddam's ability to deal with unrest at home, in fact, was strengthened during the cease-fire talks at Safwan. Schwarzkopf, who went on March 1, 1991, to the Safwan meeting uninstructed by Washington and whose primary concern was to secure the release of allied POWs, acceded to an Iraqi request that the Iraqi military be allowed to fly helicopters in southern Iraq, a measure

Iraqi generals insisted was needed because allied planes had destroyed so many bridges. The Iraqis later used the helicopters to press their attacks on the Shia uprising in southern Iraq.

Only after the 2003 invasion did the CIA learn that Saddam's regime had been so worried about losing its grip on the south that Iraqi helicopters were ordered to attack Shia rebels with Sarin nerve gas near Karbala and Najaf. Technical problems frustrated that order, which was given when American forces were still in southern Iraq. According to the CIA-sponsored Iraq Survey Group, which went to Iraq after the invasion to assess Iraq's WMD programs, 12 to 32 Sarin bombs were dropped from Mi-8 helicopters. The Sarin-filled munitions did not work properly, so the Iraqi military dropped 200 bombs with tear gas instead, the report noted.[38]

Looking back at the war, Bush noted that he was trying to strike a balance between punishing Saddam and avoiding actions that would ensnare the United States in an Iraqi civil war. "It was never our goal to break up Iraq. Indeed, we did not want that to happen, and most of our coalition partners (especially the Arabs) felt even stronger on the issue," Bush noted. "I did have a strong feeling that the Iraqi military, having been led to such a crushing defeat by Saddam, would rise up and rid themselves of him. We were concerned that the uprising would sidetrack the overthrow of Saddam, by causing the Iraqi military to rally around him to prevent the breakup of the country. That may have been what actually happened."[39]

But some of Bush's closest aides have said that they wished that some decisions had been made differently. "Saddam came to us and said, 'you know communications around the country have been destroyed, and I need to be able to communicate so I need helicopters,'" Scowcroft said in an interview. "So we said fine. Then he started to use them in an offensive way, and I called Jim Baker and Colin and said, 'We can't allow this. We've got to shut down these helicopter flights,'".[40] As it happened, there was little support in the Bush Administration for overruling Schwarzkopf. "I think that was a serious mistake," Scowcroft added. "I think one of the things that could have been different is that Saddam could have had his hands fuller than he did with trying to keep the pieces together."

Baker has a somewhat different view. Looking back on the decision, Baker said he thought it was probably a mistake to allow the Iraqis to fly helicopter attacks against the Shia in the months after the war. But Baker said he does not believe that stopping the flights would have fundamentally altered the military situation in Iraq or enabled the rebellion to be more successful. Baker also said the United States should have required Saddam to come to Safwan to sign the surrender document. In his paper on war termination, Haass had written that one objective was to ensure that Saddam was not able "to portray himself as a victor—in the Nasser manner in the midst of defeat."[41]

In the months following the war, Saddam's ability to retain control continued to preoccupy the White House. In an April 20, 1991, meeting at Camp David with Turkish Prime Minister Turgut Özal, Bush made clear that he was still looking for ways to topple Saddam without involving the United States in the internecine fighting in Iraq. "We have to get him out. He cannot remain," Bush said, according to a White House transcript of the session. "I have been wary about a war crimes tribunal because people would then want to know how we can get him. We don't want to go into Baghdad to get him."[42]

Four days later Bush told the President of the East African nation Djibouti, Hassan Gouled Aptidon., that he was concerned about reports that Iraqi forces were repressing the Shi'ites in Basra and threatening the Kurds. "We feel a responsibility," Bush said.

> It was never our intention to go in to get Saddam Hussein. World opinion sees this fear. Some are urging us to do more. I want to stop the death of babies. Saddam is making it difficult. We are helping the refugees. But it requires enormous amounts of money. We will do what is both human and right. That is the need. We are not talking about instant democracy in Baghdad, but an end to the suffering.[43]

Two weeks later, Bush returned to the subject in a phone conversation with Mubarak. The President was searching for answers shy of sending troops back into Iraq. "I wish we could get this Saddam Hussein thing laid to rest, and there is a lot of difficulty with this Kurdish situation," said Bush. "We will continue our policy and have spent lots of money but I don't want to bog down our forces."[44]

As the months went by, the frustration with Saddam's ability to cling to power continued—and not just on the part of the Americans. In a November 19, 1991, meeting Prince Bandar bin Sultan, the Saudi ambassador to Washington, delivered a message to Bush from King Fahd. It was all well and good to focus on the Arab-Israeli peace process, but the United States should not forget about Saddam. From the Saudi perspective, the outcome was far from ideal. A wounded, angry regime was still in power in Baghdad. "We have a lot to do to finish with Iraq," Bandar said, passing on King Fahd's concerns.

"Tell him not to worry," Bush replied. "We must do whatever it takes to get rid of the guy. Tell him we are not changing a bit. We are talking about ways of undermining him. There will be no letting up on sanctions or inspections. We are looking into what we can do with broadcasts. We will not go back to the status quo ante."

"Limited attacks are not enough," Bandar interjected. "His pain threshold is high. We must hit him where it hurts, at his personal security. The more we chip away at his sovereignty the better."[45]

The United States, Britain, France, and Saudi Arabia later imposed a no-fly zone in southern Iraq to stop Iraqi forces from conducting air strikes with fixed wing planes and helicopters against the Shia.[46] It was one more in a series of efforts to step up military pressure on Saddam's regime and his presumed programs to develop weapons of mass destruction that continued into the Clinton Administration. But the opportunity to maximize the pressure on the regime had long passed.

The 2003 invasion of Iraq would later be described as a "war of choice," which it was. In 2002, the United States was, in fact, faced with a choice. To achieve its goals of shutting down Iraq's presumed weapons of mass destruction programs, the United States might have tried to shore up the fraying sanctions regime, and perhaps couple that with occasional bombing raids, which was the policy of the George H. W. Bush Administration and Clinton Administration. Alternatively, it had the option of using American military might to overthrow Saddam's regime. But it was the 1991 war that framed this choice, and it is difficult to imagine that there ever would have been an American invasion of Iraq in 2003 if the earlier conflict had not occurred. It was Saddam's refusal to fully comply with the terms of the disarmament resolutions that the UN Security Council imposed after Desert Storm that kept Iraq on the UN docket and which provided Bush with his formal casus belli.

In the months after the 1991 war, the White House sought to use political, economic, and even military pressure to undermine

Saddam's hold on power. And yet by declaring an end to the ground war at 100 hours, allowing the Iraqi military to fly helicopter strikes against Shia rebels, and quickly removing American forces from southern Iraq, the Bush Administration failed to maximize pressure on the regime when it had the greatest chance of undermining the Iraqi leader's grip on power, which though not a formal war aim was an important presidential objective. The 1991 war was an impressive victory but not as great as it might have been.

III

One of the most important legacies of the 1991 Gulf War is the way in which it influenced each side's military strategy for the war that was to come. By his own account, Saddam was surprised by the Shia uprising that followed the Desert Storm campaign. "I never expected that some of our people, a small number, would betray us," he told his aides a year after the war. "I thought that it would never happen."[47] While Saddam credited Iraqi pilots with putting down much of the Shia unrest, he was determined to do what he could to prevent a repeat. "The summary of our analysis is that an Arab uprising is more dangerous than a Kurdish uprising," Saddam said at a February 9, 1998, meeting he held with his Revolutionary Command Council. "The Kurdish issue cannot extend to all of Iraq, but any Arab issue can extend to all of Iraq."[48]

In the immediate aftermath of the Shia rebellion, Iraqi officials analyzed the cause of the revolt and came up with several recommendations that might have been contained in an American counterinsurgency manual. The rioting, concluded a study carried out jointly by Basra University and the Southern Region Intelligence Director, asserted that the violent opposition to the government did not represent the attitude of most of the Iraqi public and was encouraged by Iranian agents. The government, the study suggested, would secure more support from a restive public by reducing unemployment and controlling the prices of food and basic goods.[49]

The main response, however, was military. Paramilitary organizations like the Saddam Fedayeen, Ba'ath Party Militia, and Al-Quds Force grew. The organizations reported to Saddam's regime and their role was largely geared toward internal security. Networks of safe houses and arms caches, including materials for making improvised explosives, were established throughout the country.[50] If the Shia or Kurds mounted another rebellion, the paramilitary forces were to fight the insurgents until the Iraqi Army and Air Force could be brought in to quash the insurrection. The Hostile Activities Directorate of Iraq's intelligence service was also reorganized and focused on a variety of internal religious, sectarian, and nationalist groups.[51]

Saddam also decided to work with the tribes, some of which had participated in suppressing the 1991 rebellion. "We need to make people feel that they are our people and therefore these people will fulfill their duties without receiving any instructions from us," Saddam said in a February 1992 meeting with his commanders. Saddam and his aides decided that it would be asking too much to try to disarm the tribes and that they should instead be allowed to keep weapons as long as they worked with the regime. Seeking to gain a measure of control over the tribes, Saddam and his aides discussed registering the serial numbers of the arms that would be distributed to favored tribes. There was a synergy to Saddam's policy as favored tribal officials were appointed to senior posts in the regime's security organizations.[52]

As for the United States, Saddam and his inner circle saw it as a lesser danger than internal instability and Iran. Saddam comforted himself with the thought that American power was waning. In a 1991 meeting between Saddam and tribal leaders, Saddam asserted that the United States' determination to assemble a broad coalition, including oil-rich Arab nations, for its Desert Storm campaign indicated that it lacked the ability to act alone. "They waited until 30 countries joined and then they attacked," Saddam said. "They are celebrating the event to erase the memories of Vietnam. Don't you think they were very lucky?"[53]

The United States' advantages in the air and its superior military technology, Saddam's regime concluded in one of the many official lessons he circulated after the war, masked a fear of urban combat. "Clinging to cities is necessary to protect units from sudden strikes and to force the enemy to engage in urban combat, in which it will sustain heavy losses," it noted. "The enemy has no tolerance for serious losses, especially in human lives."[54] When the United States intervened in Somalia and suffered losses in Mogadishu, Saddam again concluded that American power was overextended and in decline.[55] Saddam also discounted the possibility that the United States would arm and equip the Shia, noting correctly that American policy did not welcome the breakup of Iraq and the establishment of an independent Shia state.[56]

As 2003 approached, the array of dangers looked different in Baghdad than it did in Washington. Saddam and his generals remained concerned about Iran, so much so that the regime was reluctant to be transparent about the status of its nonexistent stocks of chemical and biological weapons, and its frozen nuclear weapons program. Saddam's strategy was to comply with the letter of the UN inspections, but not fulfill the spirit of the demands, in the hope that this would preclude the UN Security Council from authorizing a military action while maintaining a degree of ambiguity over Iraq's WMD efforts to deter adversaries in the region—a strategy Lieutenant General Raad Majid al-Hamdani, the commander of the Second Republican Guard Corps, referred to as "deterrence by doubt."[57]

As it became clear that a gridlocked Security Council would not prevent the Americans from attacking, Saddam prepared for the danger that had rocked his regime in 1991: a Shia rebellion. The paramilitary units Saddam had established were to hold the line against Shia insurgents if they sought to take advantage of the conflict to rise up again. To make it easier to reinforce the para-military units with Iraqi Army units, Saddam issued instructions that no bridges were to be destroyed without his explicit approval. The regime recalled how the American air strikes on bridges had hampered its effort to suppress the Shia in 1991 and calculated that they would need the spans to send troops south if the Shia again rebelled.

As for the American threat, Saddam anticipated a punishing air campaign. The regime moved the furniture from Saddam's palaces into a nondescript building and tagged it so it could be moved back after the conflict was over. American ground forces had refrained from moving on the Iraqi capital in 1991 when the United States had far more troops and the Iraqi army was on the run. In the months leading up to the 2003 war Saddam did not seem persuaded that the United States had the will and means of successfully taking Baghdad. "Two or three months before the war, Saddam Hussein addressed a group of 150 officers," the direc-tor of Iraqi military intelligence told US interrogators, "Saddam and his inner circle thought the war would last a few days and then it would be over. They thought there would be a few air strikes and maybe some operations in the south, then it would be over."[58]

Preparations were made to defend the Iraqi capital. Baghdad was ringed with Republican Guard divisions. But Saddam calculated that American forces would have a difficult time if they decided to drive north. The regime assumed that the American forces would need to battle their way along heavily defended north-south highways and southern Iraqi cities.[59] It discounted the possibility that many of the American ground forces could bypass major urban centers and byways as they advanced. The most likely way Americans could quickly approach Baghdad, Saddam's generals thought, was an airborne operation to seize Saddam International Airport. To fend off that threat, Iraqi soldiers dug in at the airport, their guns pointing up.[60]

The American-led coalition also tended to fight the last war. American commanders assumed that the main enemy was the Republican Guards forces, the supposedly elite troops the United States had sought to crush in 1991. Chemical and biological weapons, which Iraq had in abundance in 1991, were also rated a major danger. Baghdad was considered to be the "center of gravity." Once the Republican Guards were defeated, the capital was captured, and the regime's ministries brought under control, the American command thought the war would be won.

Assuming that Iraq's conventional forces represented the main threat, American commanders failed to understand how Saddam had modified his strategy to put down a Shia rebellion. They neither prepared to fight the paramilitary forces that had been dispersed throughout southern Iraq nor understood that they might emerge as the nucleus of an insurgency once the regime was ousted. The Pentagon provided enough forces to topple the regime but not enough to secure the country or deprive insurgents of a potential sanctuary in Anbar province and other parts of Iraq.

CIA officers also made their share of mistakes. Assuming that the Shia would rise up as they had in 1991 and welcome the American liberators, some operatives hatched a plan to distribute tiny American flags in towns like Samawah and Nasiriyah so that the residents could welcome the American invaders and perhaps march with them in parades. Fortunately, the plan was blocked by the American military, which did not want to flaunt the American role.

The collision of the Iraqi and American strategies produced surprises for each side. The Shia were stung by the refusal of the United States to come to their aid in 1991 and were fearful of rising up against the regime again, as many American military and intelligence officials had anticipated. During the early weeks of the war, the Shia did little to challenge Saddam or help the Americans.

The American military was also surprised to encounter Saddam's paramilitary forces as they headed north, and the irregular units became such a threat to American supply lines that American commanders decided to pause their attack briefly. The Americans resumed the march toward Baghdad, but rare was the intelligence officer who noted that the American-led coalition was merely bypassing fighters that it would need to confront again. An exception was Joseph Apodaca, a Marine lieutenant colonel who was an expert on counterinsurgency in Latin America. Apodaca drafted a classified assessment that compared the Saddam Fedayeen attacks to the insurgencies in Nicaragua, El Salvador, and Colombia, pointing out the similarities and differences. Unless the American-led coalition chased after the Saddam Fedayeen in Iraq's smaller towns and villages their attacks on the allies and Iraqi infrastructure would continue, hampering efforts to stabilize Iraq. The classified memo was sent up the chain of command with no appreciable effect on American military planning.[61]

As American forces continued their advance, Lieutenant General Raad al-Hamdani, the commander of the II Republican Guard Corps was able to persuade Saddam to make an exemption so that he could blow up the al-Kaed bridge, a critical span over the Euphrates that provided a route to Baghdad. But the move came late and the US Army's 3rd Infantry Division was able to get across the Euphrates before the bridge was destroyed.[62]

As the Americans seized Baghdad, the remnants of the regime fought for its survival. Lieutenant General David McKiernan, the land war commander, wanted to deploy the 1st Cavalry Division and dispatch it to Anbar, the western Sunni province, which became a hotbed for the insurgency. But as it became clear that the regime would fall, Rumsfeld pressured General Tommy Franks, the CENTCOM commander, to "off-ramp" the division and it was never sent. It was one of the early mistakes of the war and stemmed from the inability to understand the nature of the conflict and how it might evolve. The limited number of troops also made it difficult for the Americans to monitor the borders and restrict the infiltration of foreign fighters.

The paramilitary units Saddam had enlisted to wage a counterinsurgency campaign in the event of a Shia or Kurdish rebellion found themselves with a network of arms caches, safe houses, and the technical expertise to stage attacks on the United States and allied forces. The relationships with Islamist organizations and terrorist groups that Saddam had established to keep an eye on the potential threats to his rule became a means of importing jihadists and suicide bombers.[63]

The decree by L. Paul Bremer, the head of the Coalition Provisional Authority, to disband the Iraqi army and slowly build a new force from scratch was intended to rid the new Iraq of Saddam supporters and ensure that the Iraqi military could not intervene in politics. But the move, which was outlined in advance to Rumsfeld, increased the pool of alienated and, in many cases, well-trained potential recruits for the nascent insurgency. Bremer's decision to take a broader approach toward de-Ba'athification than many US military officers, intelligence experts, and British officials favored had a similarly counterproductive effect.

The transformation of the regime's defensive counterinsurgency strategy to suppress a domestic rebellion into an offensive anti-American insurgency would eventually be deciphered by American intelligence. But by then a long, difficult war was underway.

[5]

THE ARAB DIMENSION OF SADDAM HUSSEIN'S CALCULATIONS: WHAT WE HAVE LEARNED FROM IRAQI RECORDS

Shibley Telhami

Two decades after an American-led international coalition dislodged the Iraqi army from Kuwait, a great public awakening swept through the Arab world, toppling some of the longest-serving rulers in the region and threatening others. Saddam Hussein had been toppled eight years earlier by another American-led campaign and executed later by the new rulers in Baghdad. Whether the Arab Spring of 2011 would have toppled his regime had he endured is impossible to know. But the Arab public empowerment that the Iraqi ruler had counted on as a deterrent against foreign intervention—and which had failed him in both wars—finally arrived. It was a reminder of something that had been little understood about Saddam Hussein and his miscalculations in invading Kuwait: much of his calculus pertained to Arab public opinion and its impact on the behavior of Arab and foreign rulers. This interpretation is only reinforced by new archival materials from his era.

More than twenty years after the Iraqi invasion of Kuwait, it is still difficult to state with certainty the exact point at which Hussein contemplated invading his southern neighbor. Much of the literature has focused on the economic crisis that Iraq faced on the eve of the invasion, which undermined the Iraqi leader's grand ambitions, on the border dispute with Kuwait, and on general Iraqi frustration with Kuwaiti policies. In the years since the war, there has been much to support the import of these variables, including records of conversations between Saddam Hussein and his closest aides now available to scholars.

And yet, while there is no smoking-gun evidence, there is circumstantial evidence that Hussein was expecting a crisis, possibly war with the United States, months before he invaded Kuwait. And the new evidence from the records of meetings with his advisers and with foreign leaders portray a leader with limited information about the outside world and with a worldview that is seemingly contradictory: on the one hand, he sees a fully empowered America in the post-Cold War era, and, on the other hand, he envisions an ability to stop it. On the one hand, he sees a weakened Soviet Union, and, on the other hand, he hopes it will somehow act to stop the United States.

The new material also provides clues to the worldview of a leader of Iraq whose audience was always far beyond Iraq's borders, in the larger Arab world. It suggests that Saddam Hussein anticipated and prepared for a crisis with the United States long before his August 1990 invasion of Kuwait. And it offers no evidence supporting the claim that his decision to invade was significantly affected by an absence of American resolve, or by his meeting with former US Ambassador to Iraq, April Glaspie. There is no evidence to support the theory that Saddam thought he received a green or yellow light from the United States, and much evidence that he expected hostile American reactions to his actions.

Hussein's motivation is not at issue. If he had succeeded in swallowing Kuwait, he would have at once resolved his immediate financial crisis, hugely expanded his oil exports, given himself better access to the Gulf, and projected himself as the dominant power in the region, particularly as he emerged in regional minds as the victor of the Iraq-Iran war. Given historic Iraqi claims to Kuwait that ran deep among Iraqis—and an attempt to take over Kuwait by Iraq forty years before Saddam's invasion—with some sympathy among other Arabs, the lure of the prospect is not hard to see. Add to this a poisonous relationship between the Iraqi regime and Kuwait's rulers, and the sense that Kuwaiti oil policy was contributing to the dramatic decline of oil prices in a manner that exacerbated Iraq's economic crisis, and Saddam Hussein's mindset becomes clearer.

The central issue is how the Iraqi leader believed he could get away with it. Thus, the debate has been less about *motives* and more about *opportunity*. Conventional wisdom about the latter has been very much tied to a notion of American deterrence failure, or even worse, inadvertently giving Saddam Hussein the green light to proceed. What I suggest in this chapter is that evidence from the Saddam tapes indicates different calculations by the Iraqi ruler that made him less sensitive to the signals the United States was sending prior to his invasion of Kuwait. While the United States may have been able to send a stronger signal against invasion, Hussein's sensitivity to that signal would have been uncertain given his own calculations. A tougher US position prior to the invasion may have also played into Saddam Hussein's hand and helped him rally Arab public opinion against the United States. The game for him centered, above all else, on Arab politics, and his miscalculations pertained more to Arab politics and public opinion than to American intentions.[1] There is much in the revealed private conversations with his close aides to support this thesis. This insight has implications for understanding politics in the Arab world in the shadow of the Arab Spring: even in the era of authoritarianism in the Arab world, when many analysts assumed that rulers like Saddam Hussein merely paid lip service to public opinion and regional attitudes, government behavior was hard to grasp without understanding the role of Arab politics and public opinion. And some of the insight gained by understanding Saddam Hussein's calculations remains relevant to the understanding of Arab politics today.

WORLDVIEW

One of the striking findings from reading the conversations between Saddam Hussein and his closest aides over nearly two decades is that the worldview he expressed privately is not substantially different from the one he expressed publicly, including his view of American foreign policy, of global politics, of the Palestinian question, and of Israel. While there are some fascinating new details, and some revealing judgments of foreign leaders from Yasser Arafat to Hosni Mubarak, his general outlook toward world politics is mostly consistent. It starts with a profound and long-standing mistrust of American foreign policy, viewed largely through the prism of the Israeli-Palestinian conflict.

Beyond Saddam Hussein's public speeches over the years, the picture that emerges from the newly released materials is one of constant suspicion of American policy objectives even while Iraq sought and gained American support for its war with Iran. As with his views on other issues, such as Arab nationalism and the question of Palestine, Hussein's public and private views of the United

States were largely consistent, especially in the months preceding the Iraqi invasion of Kuwait.

What is striking in reviewing the conversations between Saddam Hussein and his aides is his deep mistrust of the United States even in the mid-1980s, after Iraq had restored its diplomatic relations with Washington and Iraq began receiving assistance from the United States in its war with Iran. In one conversation in 1986, Hussein remarks:

> Why do you think I used to doubt the American side? I mean in the last three or four years—meaning when the war, of course, just started. I mean my doubt was not that great at the beginning of the war, but grew more and more six months after the war had started, and that is because there were some clear statements and what we did not see from them, we used to see in the general situation of the area before us. Therefore, comrades, the Americans used to supply Iran with weapons in the past.[2]

As the Iran-Iraq war drew to its end in 1988, Hussein's verdict, as summarized by Kevin M. Woods et al., was telling:

> "We have to be aware of America more than the Iranians" because "they are now the police for Iran, they will turn anything they find over to Iran." In Saddam's view, the United States tried to use not only Israel but also Iran as strategic weapons against Iraq. The United States, he thought, wanted to perpetuate the mutually destructive Iran-Iraq War as long as possible in order to weaken Iraq vis-à-vis Israel....America and Iraq restored diplomatic relations in 1984, and the United States provided Baghdad with dual-use materials and equipment, agricultural credits, and intelligence on the Iranians, but

Saddam's view of the United States as treacherous and conspiratorial persisted.[3]

Saddam Hussein's mistrust of the United States was in large part due to the fact that he saw Washington through the perspective of its policies toward the Arab-Israeli conflict. Even in the middle of his war with Iran, and very much in harmony with his public positions, Hussein privately expressed negative views of Washington. In 1985, after an Israeli operation against the Palestine Liberation Organization's headquarters in Tunis he tells his aides: "What is more difficult in the new international relations, is that a superpower like the United States declares its complete support [for Israel]. Furthermore, it justifies its support by stating that the Zionists' act is legitimate act of self-defense ... I have never been so upset over an issue, before or during the war, as much as I am over this one. I mean it suggests carelessness and humiliation to every human being, not only to every Arab."[4] This view of American foreign policy through the prism of the Arab-Israeli conflict is consistent throughout multiple episodes in the internal conversations between Saddam Hussein and his aides throughout the period from 1978 to 2001, as a recently published volume on the subject reveals.[5]

This view of American foreign policy was matched by a nearly textbook balance-of-power view of the world, at both the global and regional levels. Hussein had expressed this view best in an important speech he gave in February 1990, just months before he invaded Kuwait, at the Arab Cooperation Council summit in Amman, Jordan—in the presence of Hosni Mubarak of Egypt, Ali Abdullah Saleh of Yemen, and King Hussein of Jordan. The speech sought to paint the global and regional picture as the Cold War had come to an end and to articulate the implications for the Arabs. This speech, which I have referred to in an earlier publication, stands out as the clearest view Saddam ever publicly expressed of the way he interpreted global politics, particularly the role of the United States. It serves as a good starting point to evaluate the new information we now have from the recently available "Saddam Tapes." In the Amman speech, the Iraqi ruler put it this way: "I think we all agree that our meeting faces a special task of priority, which is indisputable: that is, the discussion and analysis of the changes in the international arena and their repercussions on our countries and the Arab nation in particular, and the world in general." Hussein then portrays a classic realist view of world politics since World War II: "Among the most important developments since international conflict in World War II has been the fact that... France and Britain, have declined, while the influence and impact of two countries expanded until they became the two superpowers... I mean that United States and the Soviet Union. Of course, with these results, two axes have developed: the Western axis under the leadership of the United States... or the East bloc under the leadership of the Soviet Union."

In Saddam Hussein's view, the implications were unmistakable:

The Zionist state has become a reality... and the Palestinians have become refugees.[6] While the imperialist Western world helped the expansionist scheme and aggression of the Zionist entity in 1967, the communist bloc sided with the Arabs in the concept of balance of interests in the context of the global competition between the two blocs, and sought to secure footholds for the East Bloc against the Western interests in the Arab homeland.[7]... The global policy continued on the basis of the existence of two poles that were balanced in terms of force... and suddenly, the situation changed in a dramatic way.... The USSR went to nurse the wounds that were inflicted on it.... It has become clear to everyone that the United States has emerged in a superior position in international politics.

Yet, in a manner consistent with some realist predictions based on balance of power politics, Hussein did not envision a unipolar world as lasting for long. Other powers were likely to balance American power:

> We believe that the world can fill the vacuum resulting from the recent changes and find a new balance in the global arena.... The forces that laid the ground for filling the vacuum and for the emergence of the two superpowers, the U.S. and the USSR, after World War II at the expense of France, Britain, and Germany can develop new forces, which we expect will be in Europe and Japan. America will lose its power just as quickly as it gained it by frightening Europe, Japan, and other countries through the continuous hinting at the danger of the USSR and communism. The United States will lose its power as the fierce competition for gaining the upper hand between the two superpowers and their allies recedes.[8]

But Hussein warned that until such time as there are new powers to balance the United States, Washington will be greatly emboldened: "However, we believe that the U.S. will continue to depart from the restrictions that govern the rest of the world throughout the next five years until new forces of balance are formed. Moreover, the undisciplined and irresponsible behavior will engender hostility and grudges as it embarks on rejected stupidities."[9]

As an example of US post-Cold War policies, Saddam Hussein specified two issues that summarized his view of American policy goals—controlling oil and helping Israel: "Recent American utterances and behaviors as far as pan-Arab security and Palestinian Arab rights to their homeland are concerned inevitably cause alarm and warrant Arab vigilance, or are supposed to evoke such a reaction on our part. One may cite recurrent statements by U.S. officials about their intention to keep their fleets in the Gulf for an unlimited period of time, and their support for an unprecedented exodus of Soviet Jews to Palestinian territory." Hussein was particularly harsh on the US plans to keep a fleet in the Gulf after the Iran-Iraq war had ended, with the end of the Iranian threat to Kuwait.[10]

Given that Saddam Hussein expected an empowered and unchallenged America that aimed to help Israel and control oil, it is impossible to understand his calculations in risking an American response to his invasion of Kuwait without reference to the Arab dimension.

THE ARAB DIMENSION BEFORE IRAQ INVADED KUWAIT

The record of Saddam Hussein's conversations with his closest advisers reinforces the view that much of his calculations and strategies were based on his view of Arab politics.[11] The first dimension of this pertains to Arab public opinion; the second is his strategy toward key Arab governments, especially Saudi Arabia and Egypt.

Whatever the sources of Saddam Hussein's ambitions toward Kuwait, his calculation of risk and his chances for success were linked to the prevailing mood in the region that afflicted the populace and the elites alike—a mood related to the end of the Cold

War and its perceived implications for the Arab-Israeli conflict. Most Arab leaders and elites did not see at the end of the Cold War a victory of democracy over dictatorship, or the victory of consensus politics over power politics. Instead, to Arabs the end of the Cold War, which signaled the decline of the Soviet Union as a major superpower, ushered in an era of American hegemony that also entailed Israel's regional hegemony.[12]

A common Arab view was summarized by Saddam Hussein in a speech to the Arab Cooperation Council in February 1990, cited above. He clearly understood his Arab colleagues' fear and apprehension about the new global political order.[13] Going beyond the typical interpretation of the end of the Cold War as inaugurating an era of US hegemony, and therefore Israeli hegemony, the Iraqi leader offered Arabs an alternative: if Arabs act jointly and consolidate their oil and financial resources, they will have to be taken seriously by the United States.

In pursuing his designs for Kuwait, the Iraqi leader had Arab public opinion behind him by early summer. At the end of the Arab summit conference held in May in Baghdad, anti-Americanism at the popular level was approaching the intensity of anti-British sentiment of the 1950s; Iraq had become the most influential Arab state; and Saddam Hussein's personal popularity had increased dramatically, despite his all too obvious shortcomings.[14] Driving Arab sentiment was the perception that the Arab-Israeli peace process was dead, the tilt to the right in Israeli politics, a US veto of a UN Security Council resolution on protecting Palestinians, a congressional resolution declaring Jerusalem to be the united capital of Israel, and the immigration of Soviet Jews to Israel. The prevailing sentiment was concisely summarized by a former Egyptian ambassador to the United States: "Arabs are sick of their governments pathetically begging the U.S. to plead with Israel to please let them have peace."[15] The official spokesman of the Islamic deputies in the Jordanian House of Representatives echoed the sentiment: "The U.S. hostility and arrogance must motivate our Arab and Islamic nation to put an end to the course of begging and capitulation that it is immersed in."[16] By the end of June 1990 following the suspension of the US-PLO dialogue, even Kuwaiti newspapers were calling on the Arabs "to adopt serious and objective stands against the US which persists in a position hostile to the Arab causes."[17] Egyptian President Hosni Mubarak also warned that "the biased U.S. positions will certainly return the region to dependence on the military option."[18]

By flaunting his military capabilities, targeting Israel, and highlighting the Palestinian question, Saddam Hussein filled the vacuum of regional despair. The popular success of Iraq's leader in exploiting Arab desperation is best illustrated by the reaction of some Muslim fundamentalists, who earlier had targeted him as an atheist enemy of Islam for his eight years of squandering the resources of two Islamic nations—Iran and Iraq—instead of using them to liberate Jerusalem. By summer, some Muslim leaders had convinced themselves that Saddam now saw the light and that his calls for Islamic Jihad were real.

Indeed, if Iraq made any miscalculation about invading Kuwait, it concerned Arab, not American reaction. The Iraqi leader had been saying for months that he expected the United States to have fewer constraints in advancing its interests now that the Soviets were out of the picture. But he believed that the United States could not succeed without Arab cooperation, and given the mood of despair and anti-Americanism in the region, he calculated, not unreasonably, that Arab governments would be reluctant to accept the deployment of American troops to attack an Arab state. Even in Washington, DC, as the possibility of an Iraqi invasion of Kuwait was considered at the end of July 1990, Arab public opinion was considered the primary obstacle to countering a potential Iraqi invasion militarily.[19] What Saddam seemed to forget, however, is that the very competition that initially concerned Arab governments with the Palestinian question would prevent Syria and Egypt from allowing Saddam to seize the reins of Arab leadership.

Capitalizing on Arab frustrations, and exploiting the issue of massive Soviet Jewish immigration to Israel as a symbol of the dangers that would follow the end of the Cold War, Saddam Hussein hosted a successful Arab summit in Baghdad in May 1990. This summit, which the Iraqi leader chaired and dominated, was telecast live in most Arab states, making Saddam even more popular.[20] Palestinian leader, Yasser Arafat concluded, "The most important thing to be said is that the latest Arab summit conference under the chairmanship of brother President Saddam Hussein has given a new Pan-Arab resurgence to our Arab nation through Iraqi ability."[21] Arab speeches at the Baghdad summit and extensive interviews with elites and government officials in several Arab nations indicate relative unanimity on the negative consequences of the end of the Cold War and on the extent of frustration with American policy toward the Arab-Israeli conflict. But there were two significant areas of difference.

The first issue on which Arab leaders did not have unanimous agreement concerned what tactics they could use to counter what was perceived to be a difficult global environment. In particular, most believed in 1990 that the world was entering an era of US dominance that would last several years. They also believed that American policy in the Middle East was primarily determined by "the Zionist lobby in Washington" and that American preeminence thus entailed Israel's regional dominance. How the Arabs could overcome these strategic drawbacks was a disputed issue. The Egyptians and the Syrians, even without mutual cooperation, believed that these disadvantages could not be reversed and that the Arabs should try to make the best of a bad situation. In essence, the argument centered on the assumption that this was no time to get on the wrong side of the United States. While the Arabs could not reverse American policy in the Middle East, they could cooperate with the United States to prevent possible disaster and to buy time until a new global political order emerged.[22]

In contrast to Egypt and Syria, the Iraqis argued that the Arabs possessed sufficient economic and military resources to enable them, if they acted collectively, to either compel American cooperation or to help in the formation of a counterweight to the United States.

The third view, held by the Jordanians and the Palestinians, was one of impending disaster that could not be prevented. To begin with, the Palestinians and Jordanians perceived the United States to be in "collusion with Israel." Yasser Arafat believed that the political initiatives of the Bush Administration were motivated by the desire to get more and more from the Palestinians, to buy time, and to kill the Intifada, without any serious intent to work toward Israeli compromise.[23]

The Jordanians shared this assessment. In addition, both Palestinians and Jordanians believed that Israel was about to embark on a war to implement the Sharon plan to turn Jordan into Palestine.[24] Arafat was anticipating that unless Arabs took serious countermeasures, Israel would launch an attack against Jordan within months, leading to the expulsion of Palestinians from the occupied territories. He was unconvinced by the argument that the Israeli public would not support such an incursion, especially given the lessons that Israelis had learned from their adventure in Lebanon. To his Arab colleagues, Arafat chanted: "Brother Arabs: The Israelis are beating the drum of war. They are beating the drum of war."[25] In short, for Arafat, disaster was imminent.

A similar sentiment was expressed by Jordanian elites and leaders about the imminent danger to the Arab nation.[26] So desperate was King Hussein at the Baghdad summit, so tragic was the manner of his televised speech, that some of his most loyal citizens felt humiliated by the King's tone. The King, a man with legendary talent for the game of survival, ended his speech with the following warning to Arab leaders: "I have talked about my country with such candor and bitterness in the hope that the day will never come in which I and my people in Jordan—men, women, children, and young men—have nothing to repeat on every lip but that painful cry by the Arab poet: 'They have lost me, and what a brave man they have lost, for he would have defended their frontiers on the evil day.' Peace be upon you."[27]

The unusually harmonious views of Yasser Arafat and King Hussein[28] further consolidated a relationship already strengthened by the Jordanian riots of April 1989 protesting against tough economic measures.[29] Jordanian analysts argued that, besides the economic factor, Jordanians were inspired by the Palestinian uprising and the perceived heroics of the people in south Lebanon.[30] The demonstrations were especially threatening to the King, since they took place almost exclusively in Jordanian, not Palestinian, communities.[31] There was a sense that, had the PLO not advised its supporters in Jordan against joining the demonstrations, King Hussein would have been in serious trouble.[32] Expecting more difficult economic times ahead, complicated by fears caused by Soviet Jewish immigration to Israel, the King sought to defuse the situation and spread the blame by holding elections. The PLO, on the other hand, had every incentive to help the Jordanian monarch survive, lest instability in Jordan give Israel an opportunity to implement the option of turning Jordan into a Palestinian state. While these evaluations of Arab positions were made before Iraq invaded Kuwait, it is striking that the eventual lineup of alliances over the Kuwait-Iraq conflict matched these earlier groupings.

The second important issue on which Arab rivalry showed itself even before Iraq invaded Kuwait was the question of leadership. On this question, both Syria and Egypt were uneasy about Iraq's new preeminence in Arab politics. Syria, Iraq's primary rival, was the only Arab state absent from the Baghdad summit, even though the Syrians, like the Jordanians and Palestinians, were calling on the Arabs to prepare themselves to face a war that Israel intended to launch.[33] During the Baghdad summit, Syrian officials privately expressed fear of "excessive" Iraqi influence in Arab affairs.[34] Similarly, Egyptian officials were concerned about the new Iraqi role. Egyptian presidential adviser Usama Al-Baz expressed concern, symbolically, that Yasser Arafat was spending too much of his time in Baghdad (thus acquiescing in the notion that Saddam Hussein was the new Pan-Arab champ). Al-Baz argued that Arafat should be persuaded to spend more time in Cairo, instead.[35]

In contrast to Egypt and Syria, the Jordanians, the Palestinians, the Yemenis, and some North Africans appeared enthusiastic about the Iraqis' new role. The wealthy Gulf Arabs seemed uncertain. These divisions among Arabs on the question of Iraqi leadership were eventually reflected in the various Arab coalitions that emerged following Iraq's invasion of Kuwait.

THE SAUDI AND EGYPTIAN FACTORS

It is clear from much of the evidence now available that Saddam Hussein's calculations toward Arab states, in particular his calculations for increasing his influence within the Gulf, focused primarily on the possible reactions of Saudi Arabia and Egypt.

Saudi Arabia was central, not only as the senior partner in the Gulf Cooperation Council, of which Kuwait was a member, and as a significant creditor of Iraq but also as a key player in a possible war. Had Saudi Arabia not allowed American ground forces on its soil, it would have been difficult to imagine a successful American war effort to dislodge Iraqi forces from Iraq. Thus, the early Saudi decision to welcome American forces after Iraq invaded Kuwait was central to the ultimate success of the American-led war effort. And that decision was in part dependent on the Egyptian position. Saudi Arabia needed Arab legitimacy to allow Western troops on Muslim holy lands, and Egypt was central in providing legitimacy; it is also improbable that Syria would have joined the international coalition had it not been for the Egyptian position. To understand this point, one has to understand that in all the polls that we have conducted, only a minority of Saudis, and generally less than in other Arab states, identify themselves as Saudis first; most identify themselves either as Muslim (a plurality) or Arab. This means that what Arabs and Muslims say or do matters for the Saudi public's assessments of what is good for Arabs and Muslims—and for judging whether their own government is doing the right thing. And no country matters more than Egypt, given that it alone has one quarter of the Arab people and a legacy of Arab leadership.

Seen from this perspective, Saddam Hussein initiated the formation of the Arab Cooperation Council that included Egypt and Iraq, the two aspiring leaders of the Arab world, as well as Yemen and Jordan—thus encompassing all non–Gulf Cooperation Council neighbors of Saudi Arabia. This was seen by analysts as a counterweight to the GCC and as a lever for Iraq to extract financial concessions from the GCC both on debt forgiveness and on the oil-border dispute with Kuwait. But there was also intended political pressure on Riyadh as the Arab Cooperation Council, if acting collectively, had the potential of bestowing or depriving Arab legitimacy to any action by Saudi Arabia.

Evidence suggests that Saddam Hussein may have understood that the Arab Cooperation Council—and certainly his invasion of Kuwait—could be perceived by Saudi Arabia as threats. This may explain his move to sign a bilateral nonaggression treaty with the Saudis that simultaneously sought to assure them that Iraq had no intention to invade them while getting their assurance not to allow attacks against Iraq from Saudi soil. Even after the Iraqi invasion of Kuwait, and the Saudi decision to allow international forces on their soil, there is evidence that Saddam Hussein understood Saudi insecurity. In a telling conversation with his closest aides in 1992, Saddam Hussein evaluated who was most responsible for the American-led military campaign to dislodge him from Kuwait. Hussein disagreed with the assessment that King Fahd of Saudi Arabia was most responsible and put it this way:

> We simply said that the first responsible person was Hosni [Mubarak]. We also said that [Saudi King] Fahd was the second responsible one, and Bush was third.... Hosni played a big role. First he was the tool behind bungling any Arab solution.... He was also the first to announce official Arab support before the world that the Arab Summit Council made the decision. That was very important. There were also the dirty intelligence games and curtailed information, which Westerners know are lies but they depend on them. They say, "President Mubarak said such-and-such a thing, and Fahd said such-and-such a thing." It was important to use Egypt's moral power in a devious way. The reason I placed Fahd in this sequence is because he had the excuse of fear, so what was Hosni's excuse? This is what I need

to understand....Fahd was next to Kuwait. He said whoever attacks Kuwait will attack us. This was possible. There is logic in what he said, but why did Hosni volunteer from behind the borders?...The main thing is, it was Mubarak and Fahd among the Arabs who brought these foreigners to attack us.[36]

From this and other records, it appears that Saddam Hussein was fully aware of King Fahd's potential insecurity, and it is likely that both the Arab Cooperation Council and the nonaggression treaty with Saudi Arabia were intended to limit the Saudi options in case of war. But there is also evidence that he was surprised by Mubarak's behavior, specifically his tilting toward the American camp following Iraq's invasion, which may have been the central element of his miscalculation, and the one that had the most potential impact on Arab public opinion. Some of this miscalculation is understandable. Egypt and Iraq had developed an increasingly cooperative relationship after Mubarak became President and began to reverse Egypt's isolation in the Arab world following the signing of the Egyptian-Israeli peace treaty in 1979. Iraq had taken the lead in opposing Egyptian President Anwar Sadat's move and in expelling Egypt from the Arab league. But the ascendance of Hosni Mubarak, and Iraq's need for Arab support in its war with Iran provided mutual opportunities to improve relations. Egypt was instrumental in helping improve Iraq's relations with the United States and the West, and Iraq helped bring Egypt back to the Arab fold. Economically, millions of Egyptian workers were employed in Iraq to replace Iraqi soldiers in the workforce, which generated significant remittances into the Egyptian economy— although this issue turned into a sour point in the relationship in 1989, as many Iraqi soldiers were demobilized after the end of the Iran-Iraq war. This created tensions and occasionally conflict between Iraqis and Egyptians, and resulted in the return of thousands of workers to Egypt.

Hussein may have also assumed that Egyptians, like many poorer Arabs, felt that the rich oil-producing Arab states were benefiting from the price paid in blood by their brethren in Egypt (the 1973 war, which resulted in the quadrupling of oil prices) and Iraq in its eight-year war with Iran—without sufficiently sharing their wealth. Another conversation between Saddam Hussein and his aides after the Iraqi invasion of Kuwait provides some insight into this issue. An aide reported to Hussein what Mubarak had been saying in private: "They put me up in the [Arab] Cooperation Council, but this is a conspiracy council. I have seen the way they talk about poverty, wealth and oil.... These folks intend to take over everyone.... This is truly a conspiracy council; I do not wish to conspire [apparently quoting Mubarak]."[37]

Another element of Hussein's miscalculation about Mubarak was somewhat surprising. It has to do with the Egyptian-Iraqi competition for leadership. From the inception of the Arab League in 1945, Egypt and Iraq have historically been the key competitors for Arab leadership. And this competition has defined patterns of inter-Arab relations over the past few decades. Although Egypt was taken out of the game following its peace treaty with Israel, it was slowly coming back and had just been readmitted to the Arab League in 1989, only months before Iraq invaded Kuwait. Iraq's role in that effort, the Egyptian workers on its soil, the mutual membership in the Arab Cooperation Council, and the emerging relationship between Hussein and Mubarak may have given the impression that the common interests of the two and their seemingly similar interpretations of the end of the Cold War were bigger than their historic competition. Certainly, there was a sense that Iraq helped restore Egypt's influence in the Arab world. This issue of competition was one that Saddam and his aides discussed after the invasion of Kuwait as they tried to understand Mubarak's moves. In a conversation on September 30, 1990, in which Saddam Hussein's aides seemed to be quoting from minutes of private conversations of Hosni Mubarak, Hussein said, "If Mubarak is imagining he is our leader, I swear to God nobody put it in his head other than us."[38] One of his aides reports, "So he [Mubarak] is saying that the problem is that we want to take the leadership role.... But I will never give up leadership, period! [apparently quoting Mubarak]."[39]

Exactly when Saddam Hussein planned to invade Kuwait remains uncertain, but there is some evidence that it was months in advance. Part of the evidence is circumstantial. His approach to Saudi Arabia: on the one hand, building a coalition of neighbors to counter them and the GCC that they led, and, on the other hand, to assure them through a nonaggression agreement. His focus on the Palestinian question and moves toward closer relations with PLO leader Yasser Arafat, toward whom Saddam Hussein had not always held warm views.[40] And the increasingly anti-American rhetoric beginning with the fall of 1989, but certainly in his important speech to the Arab Cooperation Council in February 1990. There are also conversations that may have given some hints of expected confrontations with United States. In a meeting with Yasser Arafat in April 1990, Hussein said:

As long as the small players are gone, and it is time for America to play the game directly, we are ready for it. We are ready. We will fight America, and with God's help we will defeat it and kick it out [of] the whole region, because it is not about the fight itself. We know that America has larger aircraft than we do. America has more rockets than us. But I think that when the Arab people see the action of war is real, not only talk, they will do the same and fight America everywhere. So, in order to be fair, we have to get ready to fight America. We are ready to fight when they are. When they strike, we will strike. We will strike any American troops in the Arab Gulf with our air force, and then we will state it, saying that our air force has assaulted the America bases on that day. . . . I wish America would bring its army and occupy Iraq. I wish they would do it so we can kill all Americans and sweep all of them—sweep all of them, by God.[41]

ARAB PUBLIC OPINION AFTER THE IRAQI INVASION OF KUWAIT

What is clear from the records is that Saddam Hussein's calculation pertained primarily to the Arab reactions, both publics and governments. And his miscalculations had more to do with Arab politics than American foreign policy.

While scholars continue to disagree about the relevance of public opinion to public behavior and state policy, several studies indicate that the causal links are affected by one important criterion: how the public ranks a given issue among its priorities. In the United States, for example, it has been shown that how an issue is ranked among public priorities affects how people contribute to campaign funds and how they vote. Those who rank an issue highest in their priorities are more likely to act on the basis of that sentiment and are more likely to affect policy on that issue.[42] Issue importance can explain some of the discrepancy between opinion and behavior. While most Middle East experts were correct in their estimations of the public sentiments in the Middle East during the Gulf crisis, many were wrong about public behavior. Assessing issue importance for each Arab country can be a helpful measure.

While voting behavior is hardly a useful indicator in Middle East polities, there are ways of measuring the impact of opinion on public behavior. For example, in the case of the Gulf War, one can look at public demonstrations as one indicator of the extent to which the public cared about the issue. While demonstrations in many Arab states are illegal and therefore risky, the pattern of demonstrations can be telling.

Iraq's invasion of Kuwait brought out several issues of contention for Arab public opinion. The first issue was the promise of deliverance from an unacceptable status quo, which was blamed on corrupt governments and foreign imperialism. The second question pertained to the principle of state sovereignty, clearly violated by Iraq. A third issue was the promise of economic redistribution in the Arab world. Fourth was the idea of a powerful Arab state finally able to stand up to Israel and western powers and to liberate Palestine. The fifth issue pertained to foreign intervention on Arab soil. While all these issues were present in the calculations of most Arabs, the relative weight of each issue varied across the Arab world.

To assess Arab popular behavior and the impact of that behavior on the policies of Arab states, it is especially helpful to rank these issues in light of the priorities of each Arab community. The fact that Arabs disagreed on the ranking of these issues—or disagreed on one issue, such as the danger inherent in one Arab state invading another—did not indicate fundamental disagreements on others. For example, most Arabs (with the possible exception of the Kuwaitis) were uneasy about the presence of foreign troops on Arab soil, and most hoped that the crisis could be exploited to resolve the Arab-Israeli conflict.

Clearly, the Jordanians and Palestinians, the two parties most vulnerable to possible Israeli threats, cared most about Iraq's potential in standing up to Israel and the United States, especially given their expectations of impending disaster prior to Iraq's invasion of Kuwait. The North Africans, the Yemenis, and the Sudanese—poor nations who envied the Gulf Arabs—were frustrated by what appeared to be imperial designs for Palestine and were lured by the possibility of economic redistribution and the resurgence of Arab pride. For wealthy Gulf Arabs, immediately threatened by Iraqi aggression, confronting Iraq was their primary objective.

As for the Syrians and Egyptians, the popular soul was more divided, although opinion tipped toward confronting Iraq only by strong government decisions. First, both Syria and Egypt feared Iraq's regional dominance; second, neither thought that Iraq could stand up to the United States, and both thought that they would be on the losing side if they did not confront Iraq. Third, extensive US lobbying played an important role in shaping opinion.

PATTERNS OF DEMONSTRATIONS IN THE ARAB WORLD

The patterns of reported demonstrations in the Arab world support the view that public behavior reflected the public ranking of issues.[43] In the months preceding Iraq's invasion of Kuwait, most reported protests took place in Jordan and Algeria: nine were reported in Jordan in April and May, and seven demonstrations were reported in Algeria during the same period.

The demonstrations held in Jordan were primarily related to the Arab-Israeli conflict. The protests were over Soviet Jewish immigration, the killing of several Palestinians by a lone Israeli in Reshon Lizion, and American policy toward the Arab-Israeli conflict. It is not surprising, therefore, that in the two months following the Iraqi invasion of Kuwait more demonstrations were reported in Jordan than anywhere else in the Arab world, with the linkage between the Arab-Israeli conflict and the Gulf crisis emphasized.

In Algeria, the demonstrations prior to the Gulf War focused primarily on domestic political and economic problems, with some favoring political reform, others protesting price rises. The Gulf crisis gave opposition groups in Algeria additional tools for mobilizing the masses and challenging the status quo.[44]

No demonstrations were reported in the Gulf States, and only one was reported in Egypt during the crisis. In Sudan and Yemen, where only one demonstration was reported in the four months before the crisis, fourteen demonstrations were reported in August, with the primary issue apparently being opposition to foreign intervention.

Still, despite differences in priorities, many Arabs, including Egyptians and Syrians (but probably not including the Arabs of the Gulf) felt that the defeat of Iraq would not be good for the Arabs, believed that the alliance against Iraq was an American hegemonic design, and once Iraqi forces came under attack, hoped for an Iraqi victory. Yet, beyond the few popular demonstrations in several Arab states, there seemed little threat to Arab governments that joined the US-led alliance against Iraq. Even more puzzling is the relatively muted popular reaction following the apparent destruction of Iraq's military force and much of its industrial base, not to mention tens of thousands of Iraqi citizens. How is this possible if Arab public opinion fits the picture described earlier?

BETWEEN PUBLIC OPINION, PUBLIC BEHAVIOR, AND STATE POLICY

There are three intervening variables linking events, opinions about them, and consequent policy. The first is the sources of public information about a given issue; the second is the ranking of that issue in public priorities; and third is the assessment of the future outcome.

As for the first issue, Iraqi leaders must have made an erroneous connection between their reading of public sentiment on the Arab-Israeli conflict and the US role in it, on the one hand, and their ability to feed that public their own version of events, on the other hand. Members of the alliance against Iraq understood from the beginning that Saddam Hussein's biggest leverage in the crisis rested on his ability to mobilize public opinion. His opponents among Arab governments were not about to make it easy for him.

In particular, Egyptian and Saudi leaders were fully aware of how Arab public frustrations (including their own people) with the state of the Arab-Israeli conflict and the perceived American support for Israel played into Saddam Hussein's hand. The more he could focus on this issue, the better for him. And the more access to the Arab public he had, the more able to tell his story, the more difficult it was going to be for other Arab governments to oppose him. His opponents had every incentive to deprive him of that leverage, even if deep down they were also frustrated by the state of the Arab-Israeli issue.

Once Egypt, Syria, and Saudi Arabia made a decision to join a US-led alliance against Iraq, they could no longer pretend they had any misgivings about United States' efforts, and they had every incentive to make a public case against the Iraqi invasion. Divided soul or not, they had to act as though the choice was utterly clear.

A coordinated information campaign portrayed a uniform picture of events.[45]

In contrast to the 1950s, the substantially enhanced capacities of these states made the task easier. More important, the appearance of a collective position among the three primary Arab actors presented an important cue for Arabs looking for external signals by which to evaluate Arab and Islamic interests. It is not surprising that Syria and Egypt, like Iraq, explained their policies in terms of Arab and Islamic interests and the cause of the Palestinians.

The information campaign deprived Iraqi leaders of extensive access to the masses they sought to mobilize. One glaring exception was the case of Jordan: Jordanian television and radio, which are monitored in the West Bank and Syria, gave people access to Iraqi views. The impact of Jordanian television on Syrian public opinion may have been critical to the formation of what many scholars and journalists believed to be a pro-Iraqi sentiment. It was probably this issue more than any other that brought Jordan under extensive criticism from the United States and its Arab allies.

To put this issue of the Arab media in perspective, 1990 preceded the satellite television revolution that followed later that decade and brought Al Jazeera TV and dozens of other new stationed that Arabs everywhere could watch. The dominant media were national and local media, most of which were there to serve the rulers' interest, in telling their side of the story, and feeding selective information while censoring others. In one striking case, the Saudi media did not initially report the Iraqi invasion of Kuwait, as such reporting would have entailed taking sides one way or the other, and the Saudi King had to decide first on how he would react to the invasion before telling the story—something that has become impossible in the era of the information revolution. And Saddam Hussein's opponents worked hard to deprive him of media access—which is why most were frustrated by Jordanian TV giving the Iraqis an outlet to air their story.

Public opinion does not automatically affect either public behavior or state policy; issue importance is a key indicator. The patterns of public and state behavior in the Arab world indicate that two measures are useful in this regard. The first is the priority rankings of the issues among the Arab governments, informed by strategic calculations; the second is the priority rankings of the issues among the Arab publics informed by the proximity of a given Arab polity to one of two conflicts—the Arab-Israeli conflict and the Persian Gulf conflict. The further removed from the Gulf that an Arab polity was, the less bothered it was by the violation of Kuwaiti sovereignty; the closer it was to the Arab-Israeli conflict, the more supportive it was of Iraq, in the hope of linkage.

Indeed, one interesting feature in the evolution of Arab public opinion is that, once the war was over and international intrusions into Iraq increased, Arab public opinion in states like Egypt, where the pro-Iraqi sentiment was muted before the war, became more sympathetic to Iraq. The liberation of Kuwait removed the primary justification for opposing Iraq but left all the elements that had brought Iraq sympathy even among its opponents. In particular, resentment of American foreign policy, particularly the presence of American troops and support for Israel were resented and Hussein could again exploit that resentment. And pervasive sympathy with the sufferings of the Iraqi people from the effects of the resulting sanctions became an issue. Even friendly Arab governments advised the United States to remove the economic sanctions throughout the 1990s.

The opposite was true among those who were the strongest supporters of Iraq (Palestinians, Jordanians, and North Africans) in the early days after the war: the devastating defeat of Iraq, while it remains a serious source of resentment, stifled public opposition. Two factors account for this: the new image of Saddam Hussein as a leader who let them down and the movement toward an Arab-Israeli peace in the 1990s. American and Arab policymakers understood that part of Saddam Hussein's popularity in the Arab world stemmed from his promise to deliver militarily what his colleagues could not do through diplomacy: justice for Palestinians and Arab independence from foreign influence. But they believed that support based on such a promise would dissipate when it appeared to have been a hoax; people generally do not support losers. Saddam's failure, despite what now appears to have been real military potential, led many to blame him for the failure, immediately after the war.

The United States' active role immediately after the war in seeking a settlement to the Arab-Israeli conflict raised hopes for a peaceful settlement of the very conflict that the Iraqi leader used to rally support. Adding to the relative quiet of the Arab public was the fact that key Arab states appeared to be coordinating their policy and going along with this process; the external cue for most Arabs was the collective Arab position—an element that also contributed to the relative public quiet during the war (since Syria, Egypt, and Saudi Arabia were all on the same side). This trend reversed, however, after the collapse of the Israeli-Palestinian negotiations in 2000, and the 2003 Iraq war.[46]

ARAB PUBLIC OPINION SINCE DESERT STORM

In October 2011, I conducted a public opinion poll in Saudi Arabia. As is the case each year with an annual Arab public opinion poll, I

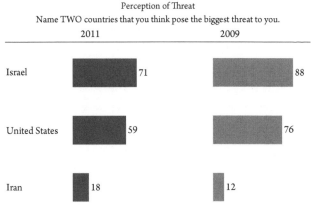

Figure 5.1

asked what leader Saudis admired most in the world, outside their own country, without providing any names. The outcome was surprising: Saddam Hussein out-polled any other world leader. Another poll next door in Jordan conducted the same month also showed Saddam Hussein nearly tied with the popular Prime Minister of Turkey, Recep Tayyip Erdogan for first place. Keeping in mind that this was also a period of talk about the rising Iranian nuclear threat, increasing Iranian influence in Iraq (which may partly explain the longing for Saddam in the two Sunni-majority states), there was another startling outcome: as noted in figure 5.1, when asked which countries posed the biggest threat to them, both Saudis and Jordanians (as well as all other Arabs we poll annually) identified Israel first, the United States second, and Iran far behind.

There was another finding that was indicative of the prevailing public attitudes. Attitudes toward the United States had been consistently negative in every Arab country throughout the previous decade, and 2011 was no exception. The evidence showed

United States & the Middle East

Which TWO of the following factors do you believe are most important in
driving American policy in the Middle East?

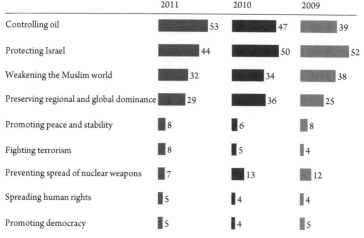

	2011	2010	2009
Controlling oil	53	47	39
Protecting Israel	44	50	52
Weakening the Muslim world	32	34	38
Preserving regional and global dominance	29	36	25
Promoting peace and stability	8	6	8
Fighting terrorism	8	5	4
Preventing spread of nuclear weapons	7	13	12
Spreading human rights	5	4	4
Promoting democracy	5	4	5

Figure 5.2

that much of that negativity centered on American policy toward
the Palestinian-Israeli conflict, and the 2003 Iraq war. But the
seeds may have been planted in 1991: asked what two steps would
improve their views of the United States most, "withdrawal from
the Arabian Peninsula" was about tied for first choice with "bro-
kering Arab-Israeli peace" and "withdrawal from Iraq." This
was roughly the same result in other countries polled (Egypt,
Morocco, Jordan, Lebanon, and the United Arab Emirates). By
2011, as Figure 5.2 demonstrates, controlling oil as an objective of
American foreign policy slightly trumped "helping Israel" in Arab
public perceptions.

The American military presence in the Gulf region following
the 1991 war appears to have reinforced Arab fears of western
domination, and there is much evidence in the polls in the past

decade to support that conclusion.[47] And a decade of strict international sanctions, unpopular in the Arab world, added to Arab public resentment.[48] It is also not a coincidence that the initial rise of Al-Qaeda in the early 1990s was rhetorically tied to the American military presence in the region following Desert Storm. While Al-Qaeda has thankfully become a shadow of itself a decade after the 9/11 tragedy, the causes that have fueled recruits over the past two decades are alive and well and may have also partly fueled the Arab public uprisings twenty years later.

The seeming de-emphasis on foreign policy issues, at least in the early months of the Arab Spring in Tunisia and Egypt, was sometimes interpreted to imply that the basic drive for freedom, democracy, and dignity in the era of the Arab public awakening lay primarily in the relationship between the rulers and the ruled and in economic conditions, including the expansion of youthful and unemployed populations in much of the region. While the latter are undoubtedly factors in the pervasive popular anger in the Arab world, it is impossible to divorce the Arab aspirations for dignity and freedom from foreign policy issues; in Arab public eyes, the very authoritarianism people despise is itself a function of a political order of foreign control that has manifested itself in varying forms from the time of the disintegration of the Ottoman Empire following World War I. And the two issues of focus have always been the Arab-Israeli conflict and the global, especially western interest in oil in the Gulf.

Neither the Arab Spring nor the pursuit of alternative energy sources are likely to reduce the importance of the Gulf region as an energy source, as even optimistic projections expect rising demand for oil well into the twenty-first century. And regardless of where Americans and others buy oil, we are all sipping from the same cup and there is only that much oil globally; the Gulf region has the lion's share of the oil reserves. The United States in particular will face choices as Asian, particularly Chinese interests in the region expand, and as global power is redistributed. How America performs in protecting its interests will depend even more today on understanding the sources of public sentiments in the region that have been central to understanding regional politics even in Saddam Hussein's era—but are even more central in the era of the information revolution and the great Arab public awakening.

NOTES

Chapter 1

1. Literature on the Gulf War abounds, with much written on military aspects of the conflict, and comparatively less available on the diplomacy behind the war, or longer historical trends through which the Gulf War passed. Contributors to this book have produced what must be ranked among the best of introductions to the conflict, including Lawrence Freedman and Ephraim Karsh, *The Gulf Conflict, 1990–1991* (Princeton: Princeton University Press, 1995); Lawrence Freedman, *A Choice of Enemies: America Confronts the Middle East* (New York: Public Affairs, 2009); Richard Haass, *War of Necessity, War of Choice: A Memoir of Two Iraq Wars* (New York: Simon & Schuster, 2010); Michael Gordon and Bernard Trainor, *The General's War: The Inside Story of the Conflict in the Gulf* (New York: Back Bay Books, 1995); and Shibley Telhami, *The Stakes: America in the Middle East* (New York: Basic Books, 2003).

2. For "emotional guy," see *Public Papers of the President George H. W. Bush,* "Remarks and Question and Answer Session with Reporters on the Relaxation of East German Border Controls," November 9, 1989. Hereinafter *PPP* with title and date. For "dance on the wall," see David Halberstam, *War in a Time of Peace: Bush, Clinton, and the Generals* (New York: Scribner, 2001), p. 10 and David Reynolds, *America, Empire of Liberty* (New York: Basic Books, 2009), p. 433.

3. Jeffrey Gray, "A Gulf Parade with Six Tons of Ticker Tape," *New York Times,* June 6, 1991, p. B1.

4. William Safire, "76 Trombones," *New York Times*, June 10, 1991, p. A17. For Bush, see *PPP*, "Radio Address to the United States Armed Forces Stationed in the Persian Gulf Region," March 2, 1991.

5. For a classic statement of the Cold War as a stabilizing force in international relations, see John Lewis Gaddis, *The Long Peace: Inquiries into the History of the Cold War* (New York: Oxford University Press, 1989). For "tempting" and "settle," see Michael Beschloss and Strobe Talbott, *At the Highest Levels: The Inside Story of the End of the Cold War* (New York: Little, Brown, and Company, 1993), p. 109.

6. For discussion of Bush's "new world order" speech, and his rhetoric more broadly, see Martin J. Medhurst, ed., *The Rhetorical Presidency of George H. W. Bush* (College Station: Texas A&M University Press, 2006) and specifically, Roy Joseph, "The New World Order: President Bush and the Post-Cold War Era," in ibid., pp. 81–101.

7. William Faulkner, *Requiem for a Nun* (New York: Vintage Books, 1975).

8. George P. Schultz, *Turmoil and Triumph: My Years as Secretary of State* (New York: Charles Scribner's Sons, 1993), p. 1131. For discussion of the end of the Cold War, in Eastern Europe and Berlin especially, see Gail Stokes, *The Walls Came Tumbling Down: Collapse and Rebirth in Eastern Europe*, 2d ed. (New York: Oxford University Press, 2011); and Jeffrey A. Engel, ed., *The Fall of the Berlin Wall: The Revolutionary Legacy of 1989* (New York: Oxford University Press, 2009).

9. Jesus Jones, "Right Here; Right Now," *Doubt* (SBK Records, 1991). The song reached No. 2 on the American charts, though ironically climbed only to No. 31 in the band's home. For discussion, see Jeffrey A. Engel, "'A Better World...But Don't Get Carried Away': The Foreign Policy of George H. W. Bush Twenty Years On," *Diplomatic History* 34, 1 (January 2010): 31 and J. Simon Rofe, "Review of Special Forum: Reconsidering the Foreign Policy of the First Bush Administration, Twenty Years On," *H-Diplo Roundtable Review* 11, 25 (2010): 9–12.

10. Veteran American diplomat Dennis Ross later recalled, "[Soviet diplomat Sergey] Tarasenko said, 'I want to find out what's going on.' I expected him to pick up the phone and call his people and he turned on the TV to get CNN. During the Gulf War there was always, CNN had this clip of [Egyptian President Hosni] Mubarak saying, 'I was always watching the CNN.' It could have been us. I could have done the clip for them." See Miller Center of Public Affairs Presidential Oral History Project, Interview with Dennis B. Ross, August 2, 2001.

11. Bush Library, NSC Papers, Doug Paul Papers, File: China-US, January-July 1989 [2], From AmEmbassy Beijing to Secstate, July 12, 1989.

12. Beschloss and Talbott, *At the Highest Levels*, p. 109.

13. "Gorbachev Takes on Congressional Leaders," *San Francisco Chronicle*, June 2, 1990, p. 1.

14. For Thatcher, see Michale Binyon, "Thatcher told Gorbachev Britain did not want German reunification," *Sunday Times*, September 11, 2009, http://www.timesonline.co.uk/tol/news/politics/article6829735.ece, accessed July 11, 2011. See also Svetlana Savranskaya et al., eds. *Masterpieces of History: The Peaceful End of the Cold War in Europe* (New York: Central European University Press, 2010), p. 532. For "deepest desire," see Andrei Grachev, *Gorbachev's Gamble: Soviet Foreign Policy & the End of the Cold War* (Malden, Mass.: Polity Press, 2008), p. 199.

15. For Scowcroft, see David Hoffman, "Gorbachev Seen as Trying to Buy Time for Reform," *Washington Post*, January 23, 1989, p. A9. For Gates, see his *From the Shadows: The Ultimate Insider's Story of Five Presidents and How They Won the Cold War* (New York: Simon & Schuster, 1996). For Cheney, see *PPP*, "Remarks at the Swearing-in Ceremony for Richard B. Cheney as Secretary of Defense," March 21, 1989.

16. Bush Public Papers, "The President's News Conference in Brussels," December 4, 1989.

17. For "look at the world," see *PPP*, "News Conference of President Bush and President Mikhail Gorbachev of the Soviet Union," June 3, 1990. Bush Library, NSC Papers, Presidential Memcons and Telcons, Meeting with Helmut Kohl, February 24, 1990, and Telephone Conversation with Margaret Thatcher, February 29, 1990.

18. James Sheehan, "The Transformation of Europe and the End of the Cold War," in Engel, *The Fall of the Berlin Wall*, p. 60.

19. For fuller discussion of Gorbachev's international vision, including his calls for a "common European home," see William Taubman and Svetlana Savranskaya, "If a Wall Fell in Berlin and Moscow Hardly Noticed, Would it Still Make a Noise?," in Engel, ed., *The Fall of the Berlin Wall*, 69–95.

20. For "end of history," see Francis Fukuyama, *The End of History and the Last Man* (New York: Free Press, 2006). Works on democratic peace theory abound. Useful primers include Bruce Russett, *Grasping the Democratic Peace* (Princeton: Princeton University Press, 2003); David R. Weart, *Never at War: Why Democracies Will Not Fight One Another* (New Haven: Yale University Press, 2001); and Michael Brown, ed., *Debating the Democratic Peace* (Cambridge, Mass.: MIT Press, 1996). For "freedom works," see *PPP*, "George H. W. Bush Inaugural Address," January 20, 1989.

21. Hal Brands and David Palkki, "'Conspiring Bastards': Saddam Hussein's Strategic View of the United States," *Diplomatic History*, 36, 3 (June 2012): 625–659. My thanks for Brands and Palkki for offering an advance copy of this essay.

22. For "we have to identify," see Kevin M. Woods, *The Mother of All Battles: Saddam Hussein's Strategic Plan for the Persian Gulf War* (Annapolis: Naval Institute Press, 2008), p. 41. For "Atlantic alliance," see Brands and Palkki.

For Hussein, see Bruce W. Jentleson, *With Friends Like These: Reagan, Bush, and Saddam, 1982–1990* (New York: W. W. Norton, 1996), p. 149.

23. For "strongly urge," see Jentleson, *With Friends Like These*, pp. 95–96. For "family of nations," employed before and after the war, see *PPP*, "Remarks at the Texas A&M University Commencement Ceremony in College Station," May 12, 1989, and after the Gulf War, "The President's News Conference on the Persian Gulf Conflict," March 1, 1991. For Gates, see Jentleson, *With Friends Like These*, p. 99.

24. For Iraqi finances, see John Ballard, *From Storm to Freedom: America's Long War with Iraq* (Annapolis: Naval Institute Press, 2010), p. 28. For discussion of NSC-26, see Jentleson, *With Friends Like These*, pp. 94–138.

25. For VOA, see Michael Palmer, *Guardians of the Gulf: A History of America's Expanding Role in the Persian Gulf, 1883–1992* (New York: Simon & Schuster, 1992), p. 156. According to Joseph Wilson, the Deputy Chief of Mission in Baghdad at the time, this broadcast was not cleared by the appropriate State Department authorities. Charles Stuart Kennedy interview of Joseph C. Wilson, "The Foreign Affairs Oral History Collection of the Association for Diplomatic Studies and Training," January 8, 2001, accessed January 10, 2010, at http://hdl.loc.gov/loc.mss/mfdip.2007wil04. For Sawyer, see http://abcnews.go.com/International/video?id=2763506, accessed July 1, 2011. For Aziz, see Woods, *The Mother of All Battles*, p. 48.

26. Brands and Palkki, "Conspiring Bastards," draft manuscript.

27. For "central post," see Woods, *The Mother of All Battles*, p. 36.

28. For Hussein and Dole, see Bush Library, NSC Papers, Richard Haass Papers, Box 43, Working Files, File: Iraq Pre 8/2/90[2], From AmEmbassay Baghdad (Glaspie) to SecState Washington, April 12, 1990. For "we will fight," see Woods, *The Mother of All Battles*, p. 51.

29. Ibid., p. 54.

30. Freedman, *Choice of Enemies*, p. 219.

31. For "kind of war," see ibid., p. 216. For "I'm Saddam Hussein," see Bush Library, NSC Papers, Richard Haass Papers, Box 43, Working Files, File: Iraq Pre 8/2/90[2], From US Embassy Baghdad (Glaspie) to Washington, July 25, 1990. Hussein's conversation with Ambassador Glaspie occurred less than a week before his invasion of Kuwait. The Iraqi leader demanded an audience with the American with such haste that she lacked time to seek specific instructions from the State Department back home. This late-night invitation was the first time in recent memory that Hussein had so privileged Washington's envoy. He rarely met with foreign diplomats, let alone for private conversations. Glaspie wisely reasoned that she could not hesitate in accepting the offer. Their conversation remains controversial to this day, for reasons described in detail below.

32. Ibid., Glaspie to Washington, July 25, 1990.

33. Ibid.

34. For "extremely bitter," see Bush Library, NSC Papers, Richard Haass Papers, Box 43, Working Files, File: Iraq Pre 8/2/90[2], Memorandum for Brent Scowcroft, through Richard Haass, from Sandra Charles, July 27, 1990, Subject: Interagency Meeting on the Persian Gulf. For "best resolved," see Bush Library, ibid., From Secstate Washington (Eagleburger) to AmEmbassy Baghdad, July 28, 1990. For "bilateral disputes," see Bush Library, NSC Papers, Richard Haass Papers, Box 43, Working Files, File: Iraq pres 8/2/90[3], From Secstate (Baker) to Various Posts, July 24, 1990, Subject: US Reaction to Iraqi Threats in the Gulf.

35. For Bush talking points, see Bush Library, NSC Papers, Richard Haass Papers, Box 43, Working Files, File: Iraq Pre 8/2/90[2], "Points to be made with Iraqi President Saddam Hussein, August 1, 1990 (NOT USED)."Glaspie's communication with Hussein prompted a media firestorm when released by the Iraqis during the war, and significant investigation and discussion later. She was not beyond criticism even from fellow long-term American Middle East experts. As Dennis Ross later recalled of the transcript, in 2001, in an oral history released only in 2011: Yes. I read it and I was just sitting there shaking my head. [Secretary of State James] Baker looked over at me and he said, "What's the matter?" I said, "Well, I'm reading this account of what April has said to Saddam Hussein. And if I were Saddam Hussein, the only conclusion I could draw from this is that basically he can go into Kuwait. We aren't going to do anything and he doesn't have to worry about anything. We're so interested in having a relationship with him, that you know, he doesn't have to worry about us at all." And he goes, "Dennis, it couldn't be that bad." So I said, "You read it." So he read it and he said, "Damn." See Miller Center Oral History with Ross, above.

36. For "summer cloud," see Woods, *The Mother of All Battles*, p. 53. For "talked to the Kuwaitis," see Miller Center for Public Affairs, George H. W. Bush Oral History Project, Interview with Thomas Pickering, December 14, 2010.

37. For "bit angry," see Bush Library, Gulf War FOIA, Haass Papers, File: Iraq Pre 8/2/90[4], Memorandum of Telephone Conversation with POTUS and King Hussein of Jordan, July 31, 1990. For "used to," see Bush Library, NSC Papers, POTUS Telcons and Memcons, Telephone Conversation with King Hussein of Jordan and President Mubarak of Egypt, August 2, 1990.

38. For "Arab unity," see Bush Library, NSC Papers, POTUS Memcons and Telcons, Telephone Call to President Turgut Özal of Turkey, August, 3, 1990. For Eagleburger, see Bush Library, NSC Papers, Richard Haass Papers, Box 43, File: Iraq—August 2, 1990-December 1990[8], Minutes of the NSC Meeting, August 3, 1990.

39. Haass, *War of Necessity*, p. 61.

40. Bush Library, NSC Papers, POTUS Memcons and Telcons, Telephone Call to President Turgut Özal of Turkey, August, 3, 1990. For Cheney, see George H. W. Bush and Brent Scowcroft, *A World Transformed* (New York: Vintage Books, 1999), pp. 316–317. Unfortunately, full minutes of this meeting remain classified at the time of this book's publication. This remains the only NSC meeting of the entire conflict still unavailable to researchers, suggesting at least that its contents might prove embarrassing to participants or detrimental to Washington's ongoing relationship with the Kuwaiti regime. We therefore have only participant memories to guide us, and the above quotes in particular derive from memoires. Bush and Scowcroft, at least, quoted above, had access to the full meeting minutes when preparing their book.

41. Pickering, Miller Center Oral History.

42. For discussion of NSC-26, see Jentleson, *With Friends Like These,* pp. 94–138.

43. Freedman, *Choice of Enemies,* pp. 102–105.

44. Janice Gross Stein, "The Wrong Strategy in the Right Place," *International Security* 13, 3 (Winter 1988–1989): 149.

45. Bush Library, Gulf War FOIA, Haass Papers, Box 43, File: Iraq Pre 8/2/90[4], From Wolfowitz to Gates, Kimmitt, Ross, and Haass, July 26, 1990.

46. Ibid.

47. *PPP,* "Remarks and Exchange with Reports on the Iraqi Invasion of Kuwait," August 5, 1990.

48. For "we can now work," see Bush Library, NSC Papers, Richard Haass Papers, Box 43, File: Iraq—August 2, 1990-December 1990[5], Memorandum of Conversation, POTUS and President Turgut Özal of Turkey, August 3, 1990. For Ross, see Miller Center Oral History.

49. *PPP,* "Joint News Conference of President Bush and Soviet President Mikhail Gorbachev, Helsinki, Finland," September 9, 1990. For Baker, see Engel, "A Better World," p. 36.

50. Christopher Maynard, *Out of the Shadow: George H. W. Bush and the End of the Cold War* (College Station: Texas A&M University Press, 2008), p. 80.

51. Bush Library, NSC Papers, Richard Haass Papers, Box 43, File: Iraq—September 1990[3], Memorandum of Conversation between POTUS and Gorbachev, September 9, 1990.

52. As Professor Carté Engel sagely notes, neither Bush nor Gorbachev could rightly claim to have invented the term "new world order." "Novus Ordo Seclorum" appeared on the great seal of the United States since 1782 and on its currency since the 1930s. While not a direct translation from this phrase, whose origins trace to Virgil, the notion of a "new world order" was hardly a late twentieth-century development. For "historic vision," see George H. W. Bush, "Address before a Joint Session of the Congress on the Persian Gulf Crisis and the Federal Budget Deficit," September 11, 1990.

53. For "opportunity," see Maynard, *Out of the Shadow*, p. x. Bush declared the Gulf War had "kicked the Vietnam syndrome once and for all." James Baker, however, believed the earlier Panama invasion played just as crucial a role in exorcising the ghosts of that quagmire. "In breaking the mindset of the American people about the use of force in the post-Vietnam era, Panama established an emotional predicate that permitted us to build the public support so essential for the success of Operation Desert Storm some thirteen months later." See George H. W. Bush, "Remarks to the American Legislative Exchange Council," March 1, 1991 and James A. Baker, *The Politics of Diplomacy* (New York: G. P. Putnam's Sons, 1995), p. 194. For discussion of Vietnam's strategic legacy for American policymakers and politicians, see Robert Schulzinger, *A Time for Peace: The Legacy of the Vietnam War* (New York: Oxford University Press, 2008).

54. Bush Library, NSC Papers, POTUS Telcons and Memcons, Telephone Conversation with President Mikhail Gorbachev, January 18, 1991.

55. Baker, *Politics of Diplomacy*, p. 313.

56. Bush Library, NSC Papers, Richard Haass Papers, Box 46, File: Iraq— February 1991[3], Bush and Gorbachev Telcon, February 23, 1991.

57. Ibid.

58. P. Edward Haley, "It Wasn't My Fault: Or, Why Saddam Surprised the Bush Administration and Invaded Kuwait," in M. Bose and R. Perotti, *From Cold War to New World Order: The Foreign Policy of George H. W. Bush* (Westport, CT: Greenwood Press, 2002), p. 110.

59. Linda J. Bilmes and Joseph E. Stiglitz, "The Iraq War Will Cost Us $3 Trillion, and Much More," *Washington Post*, March 9, 2008.

60. For "you're aware," see Baker, *Politics of Diplomacy*, p. 277. For Mitchell, see Freedman, *A Choice of Enemies*, p. 228.

61. S. H. Kelly, "Bush Tells Gulf Vets Why Hussein Left in Baghdad," http://www.fas.org/news/iraq/1999/03/a19990303bush.htm, accessed July 11, 2011.

62. James A. Baker, *Work Hard, Study...and Keep out of Politics!* (New York: G. P. Putnam's Sons, 2006), pp. 298–299.

63. For polling data, see Andrew Rosenthal, "Support for President, Amid Some Questions," *New York Times*, June 11, 1991, p. A1. Bush later quipped, in 1999, that it was "a sore spot with me, to be out of work while Saddam Hussein still has a job. It's not fair." http://www.fas.org/news/iraq/1999/03/a19990303bush.htm, accessed July 11, 2011. For Thatcher, see Peter Victor, "Thatcher Hits at Allies' Failure to Destroy Saddam," *The Independent*, January 5, 1996.

64. "US Options in Confronting Iraq," Committee on International Relations, House of Representatives, February 25, 1998, http://commdocs.house.gov/committees/intlrel/hfa48782.000/hfa48782_0.htm, accessed September 13, 2011.

Chapter 3

1. John J. Mearsheimer, "Back to the Future: Instability in Europe after the Cold War," *International Security* 15, 1 (Summer 1990).
2. There were twelve resolutions covering all aspects of the crisis in 1990, culminating in Resolution 678 of November 29 authorizing the "use of all necessary means" to implement previous resolutions. It was only in this last resolution that one of the Permanent Members (China) abstained. Those resolutions, which were largely condemnatory of Iraqi actions, were generally unanimous. In those which authorized action against Iraq, Cuba and Yemen tended to abstain or vote against. The Permanent Members worked together in the temporary and permanent cease-fire resolutions of 1991 (686 on March 2 and 687 on April 3, respectively).
3. President George Bush, Address to Congress, September 11, 1990 (US Information Service).
4. President George Bush, Speech at Air University, Maxwell Air Force Base, April 13, 1991 (US Information Service).
5. Flora Lewis, "A More Orderly World, Not a 'New World Order,'" *International Herald Tribune*, February 18, 1991. A similar but more pessimistic argument is found in Stanley Hoffmann, "Watch Out for a New World Disorder" and "A State's Internal Conditions are Outsiders' Business," *IHT*, February 26 and 27, 1991.
6. Bush observed that "I do not want one single soldier or airman shoved into a civil war in Iraq that's been going on for ages." See Maureen Dowd, "Bush Stands Firm on Military Policy in Iraqi Civil War," *The New York Times*, April 14, 1991, p. A10.

Chapter 4

1. While 148 US military personnel were killed in action, the total number of US in-theater deaths, including accidents and "non-hostile" deaths is 383. Personnel and Procurement Statistics, "Persian Gulf War Casualty Summary," United States Department of Defense, January 29, 2010, http://siadapp.dmdc.osd.mil/personnel/CASUALTY/GWSUM.pdf; for Coalition casualties, see Encarta Encyclopedia, "Persian Gulf War," Microsoft Corporation, 1993–2009, http://www.duke.edu/~asr6/Persian%20Gulf%20War.pdf.
2. Author's interview with Brent Scowcroft, May 17, 2011.
3. See Bush Library Archives: meeting with Sheikh Sabah al-Sabah of Kuwait, August 4, 1990; telephone conversation with President Turgut Özal of

Turkey, August 30, 1990; Phone conversation with King Fahd of Saudi Arabia, February 28, 1991; meeting with Hans-Dietrich Genscher, Foreign Ministry of Germany, March 1, 1991; meeting and dinner with Italian Prime Minister Andreotti, March 24, 1991; meeting with Tunisian Ambassador Ismail Khelil, April 11, 1991; and a meeting with Saudi Ambassador Prince Bandar bin Sultan, November 19, 1991

4. Michael Gordon, "Hussein Wanted Soviets to Head Off U.S. in 1991," *New York Times*, January 19, 2011, http://www.nytimes.com/2011/01/20/world/middleeast/20archive.html.

5. Michael R. Gordon and Bernard E. Trainor, *The General's War* (New York: Little, Brown and Company, 1995), p. 10.

6. The full collection of Saddam Hussein's government archives are housed at the Conflict Records Research Center (CRRC) at the National Defense University in Washington, DC. All subsequent references to this material are taken from unofficial English translations of the original Arabic text or audio files: For Saddam's reaction to the Iran-Contra affair, see a record of a meeting between Saddam Hussein and the General Command of the Armed Forces, November 1986, CRRC, SH-SHTP-D-000-608.

7. Bush Library Archives, Diplomatic Cables, October 13th, 23rd, and 24th, 1989, Peter Rodman Subject Files, 4, 18–21, and 26–27. Author's interview with James A. Baker III. June 2, 2011.

8. A copy of Dole's original letter to President Bush (dated April 17, 1990) describing his interactions with Saddam during his Baghdad visit is included as part of a series of correspondence between Dole and Brent Scowcroft from May 4, 1990 to May 15, 1990, Bush Library Archives, Peter Rodman Subject Files, 9–15.

9. Author's Interview with Edward W. Gnehm Jr., May 26, 2011.

10. Jamal Halaby, "Arab Leaders Call for Unity in Face of Worldwide Changes," *Associated Press*, February 24, 1990.

11. Author's interview with Edward W. Gnehm Jr., May 26, 2011.

12. Rick Francona, *Ally to Adversary: An Eyewitness Account of Iraq's Fall from Grace* (Annapolis: Naval Institute Press, 1999), pp. 25–26.

13. For the full memo from Embassy Baghdad to Embassy Paris, see Bush Presidential Materials, National Security Council, Bruce O. Riedel Files, Subject File Desert Storm (1) [OA/ID CF01095], 2.

14. SH-AADF-D-000-881, Iraqi Air & Air Defense Force intelligence report, July 1990, CRRC, Washington, DC.

15. Gordon and Trainor, *The General's War*, p. 16.

16. Ibid., p. 8.

17. Ibid., pp. 17–20.

18. Ibid., pp. 20–22; also see Glaspie's original diplomatic cable made public by Wikileaks.

19. Gordon and Trainor, *The General's War*, p. 26.
20. Author's interview with Brent Scowcroft, May 17, 2011.
21. Richard N. Haass, *War of Necessity, War of Choice: A Memoir of Two Iraq Wars* (New York: Simon and Schuster, 2009), p. 3.
22. State Department Diplomatic Cable, "Iraqi Incursion across Kuwaiti Border," August 2, 1990, made public by Wikileaks.
23. SH-MISC-D-000-783, Speeches of Saddam Hussein and draft copy of news article for the Iraqi state media, August 10, 1990, CRRC, Washington, DC; also see SH-SPPC-D-000-909, which is an alternate translation (both translations are unofficial).
24. See Haass, *War of Necessity*.
25. Gordon and Trainor, *The General's War*, p. 163.
26. Richard Haass, "U.S. (Coalition) War Objectives and War Termination Working Paper," Bush Library Archive, January 1991, Richard Haass Working File, 13–14.
27. Gordon and Trainor, *The General's War*, p. 190.
28. Ibid., pp. 267–288.
29. Gordon, "Hussein Wanted Soviets to Head Off U.S."
30. Ibid.; also see "The Eve of War: Four Days of Diplomacy," *New York Times Interactive* (online), January 19, 2011, http://www.nytimes.com/interactive/2011/01/20/world/middleeast/20110120-archive.html.
31. General (Ret.) Walter E. Boomer, "Lenore and Francis Humphrys International Speakers Program Event: 20th Anniversary Commemoration of the Beginning of Military Operations to Liberate Kuwait," Texas A&M University Symposium, Bush School of Government and Public Service, January 20, 2011, http://bush.tamu.edu/scowcroft/events/gulfwar20/.
32. Gordon and Trainor, *The General's War*, p. 423.
33. Boomer, "Lenore and Francis Humphrys International Speakers Program Event"; also see Rick Smith, "Remembering Desert Storm: Did It End Too Soon?" Capitol Broadcasting Company, WRAL News, January 15, 2011, http://www.wral.com/news/local/story/8946142/.
34. Gordon and Trainor, *The General's War*, p. 425.
35. Ibid., p. 429.
36. Phone conversation between President Bush and King Fahd bin Abdul Aziz Al Saud, Bush Library Archives, February 28, 1991.
37. Bet with author.
38. Michael R. Gordon and Bernard E. Trainor, *Cobra II: The Inside Story of the Invasion and Occupation of Iraq* (New York: Pantheon Books, 2006), pp. 55–57; also see "Comprehensive Report of the Special Advisor to the Central Intelligence on Iraq's WMD, with Addendums (Duelfer Report)," vol. I, Regime Strategic Intent, September 30, 2004, p. 25.
39. Gordon and Trainor, *The General's War*, p. 456.

40. Author's interview with Brent Scowcroft, May 17, 2011.

41. James A. Baker III, "Lenore and Francis Humphrys International Speakers Program Event: 20th Anniversary Commemoration of the Beginning of Military Operations to Liberate Kuwait," Texas A&M University Symposium, Bush School of Government and Public Service, January 20, 2011, http://bush.tamu.edu/scowcroft/events/gulfwar20/; also see partially declassified memo from Richard Haass titled "U.S. (Coalition) War Objectives and War Termination," Bush Presidential Library Archives, January 1990.

42. Telephone conversation between President Bush and President Özal of Turkey, Bush Library Archive, April 20, 1991, Richard Haass Working File, 22.

43. Meeting between President Bush and Hassan Gouled of the Republic of Djibouti, Bush Library Archive, April 24, 1991.

44. Phone conversation between President Bush and President Mubarak of Egypt, Bush Library Archive, May 7, 1991.

45. Meeting between President Bush and Prince Bandar bin Sultan, Bush Library Archive, November 19, 1991.

46. Michael R. Gordon, "British, French and U.S. Agree to Hit Iraqi Aircraft in the South," New York Times, August 19, 1992, p. A1.

47. SH-RVCC-D-000-610, Transcript of a meeting between Saddam Hussein and his Revolutionary Command Council, February 1992, CRRC, Washington, DC.

48. SH-SHTP-A-000-756, Unofficial transcript of a meeting between Saddam Hussein and members of the Ba'ath Party Revolutionary Command Council, February 9, 1998, CRRC, Washington, DC.

49. SH-IISX-D-000-404, Iraqi intelligence report on the 1991 rebellion titled "The Face of Treason and Treachery," October 15, 1991, CRRC, Washington, DC.

50. Gordon and Trainor, Cobra II, pp. 61–62; Kevin M. Woods, Michael R. Pease, Mark E. Stout, Williamson Murray, and James G. Lacey, The Iraqi Perspectives Report: Saddam's Senior Leadership on Operation Iraqi Freedom from the Official U.S. Joint Forces Command Report (Annapolis: Naval Institute Press, 2006), pp. 48–55. Also, from the CRRC, see SH-IISX-D-001-007, Iraqi Intelligence Service al-Ghafaki project annual report, March 14, 2000; SH-QDSA-D-000-208, Training course syllabus for the al-Quds Army, June 26, 2002; and SH-FSDM-D-000-335, A pamphlet covering the history, missions, plans, and formations of the Fedayeen Saddam, January 1, 1998.

51. SH-IISX-D-000-681, Iraqi Intelligence Services report on restructuring the Hostile Activities Directorate (M-40), September 1997, CRRC, Washington, DC.

52. SH-RVCC-D-000-610, Unofficial transcript of a meeting between Saddam Hussein and his military advisors, February 1992, CRRC, Washington, DC.

53. SH-SHTP-A-000-891, Unofficial transcript of meeting between Saddam Hussein and leaders of Saddam City, 1991, CRRC, Washington, DC.

54. SH-RPGD-D-000-490, Iraqi Republican Guard study on lessons learned from the Mother of All Battles, September 1995, CRRC, Washington, DC.

55. SH-SHTP-A-000-753, Unofficial transcript of Saddam Hussein meeting with high ranking Iraqi officials, unknown date, CRRC, Washington, DC.

56. SH-SHTP-A-000-756, Unofficial transcript of a meeting between Saddam Hussein and members of the Ba'ath Party Revolutionary Command Council, February 9, 1998, CRRC, Washington, DC.

57. Gordon and Trainor, *Cobra II*, p. 65.

58. Ibid., p. 121; "U.S. Joint Forces Command Combat Study: Iraqi Perspectives on Operation Iraqi Freedom Major Combat Operations," classified "secret." Reviewed by author.

59. Woods et al., *The Iraqi Perspectives Report*, pp. 104–105.

60. Gordon and Trainor, *Cobra II*, p. 357.

61. Ibid., p. 258.

62. Ibid., pp. 346–347.

63. SH-IDGS-D-001-106, Correspondence from Iraq's Directorate of General Security indicating that 646 volunteer fighters had crossed through Syria into Iraq, March-April 2003, CRRC, Washington, DC.

Chapter 5

1. In an article entitled "Did We Appease Iraq?" published in the *New York Times* on June 29, 1992, I hinted at this possibility, long before we knew how Saddam Hussein and his aides interpreted events privately. My argument was "U.S. policy did not mislead Iraq. Primarily, Saddam Hussein miscalculated not American but Arab reaction. He understood for months that the U.S., free of Soviet constraints, would counter his aggression."

2. Kevin M. Woods, David D. Palkki, and Mark E. Stout, *The Saddam Tapes: The Inner Workings of a Tyrant's Regime, 1978-2001* (New York: Cambridge University Press, 2011), p. 38.

3. Ibid., p. 50.

4. Ibid., p. 84.

5. Ibid.

6. The Palestinian-Israeli conflict comes out as a central prism through which Saddam Hussein viewed world politics in many of the conversations between Hussein and his aides. While some of this is clearly instrumental, depending on his audience, as is partly the case in this speech which also takes place in the midst of considerable Arab anger over the issue of planned Soviet Jewish

immigration to Israel and the expansion of Jewish settlements, there is also considerable evidence (see below) that Hussein expressed nearly identical views in purely private conversations with his closest advisers without an external audience.

7. Saddam Hussein's view of the Soviet Union, clearly expressed here, is purely a realist view, seeing Moscow primarily as a superpower trying to advance its interests around the world in the context of a balance-of-power game with the United States.

8. It is worth noting that Hussein's own view was also consistent with the view of many Western realist analysts in identifying the likely competitors with the United States at that time, which, remarkably, did not include China—perhaps because of the envisioned timeline for a new balance of power (as short as five years in Saddam Hussein's view).

9. This assessment appears particularly puzzling given that Hussein gave the United States an opportunity to test its "unrestricted power" only months after he gave this speech. I will offer my thoughts on this seeming contradiction below.

10. Saddam Hussein's references to Kuwait were noteworthy: "Iranian aggression had extended to other Arabian Gulf countries, most notably the sisterly state of Kuwait. At the time, beyond the conflicting views regarding the presence of foreign fleets in Arab territorial waters and foreign bases on their territory and their repercussions for pan-Arab security, that excessive deployment was somehow comprehensible. But now, and against the background of the recent world developments and the cessation of hostilities between Iraq and Iran, and with Kuwait no longer being the target of Iranian aggression, the Arabian Gulf states, including Iraq, and even the entire Arabs would have liked the Americans to state their intention to withdraw their fleets."

11. These sections of the article are adaptations of my article about Arab public opinion and the Gulf War, which appeared in *Political Science Quarterly* (Shibley Telhami, "Arab Public Opinion and the Gulf War," PSQ 108, 3 (Autumn 1993): 437–452).

12. The speeches by Arab leaders meeting at the Baghdad summit at the end of May 1990 are a good indicator of official views on this question. These views were also consistent among Arab elites and leaders in Egypt, Syria, Iraq, Jordan, and the West Bank in May and June 1990. This assessment is based on dozens of interviews I conducted in the region during that period in preparing a report for Representative Lee H. Hamilton, chairman of the House Subcommittee on Europe and the Middle East.

13. For an assessment of the Arab interpretation of the end of the Cold War, see Shibley Telhami, "Middle East Politics in the Post-Cold War Era," in George W. Breslauer, Harry Kreisler, and Benjamin Ward, eds., *Beyond the Cold*

War: Conflict and Cooperation in the Third World (Berkeley: IIS, University of California at Berkeley, 1992).

14. "An Anti-Zionist Ink-blot," *The Economist*, June 2, 1990, quoted an Iraqi passer-by: "Nasser made promises, but could not deliver. But when Saddam speaks, he acts." A lot of Arabs, including millions beyond Iraq, seem inclined to agree. On May 19, 1990, *The Economist* concluded that "By meeting in Baghdad, Iraq's capital, the Arabs hope to show the world that they stand fully behind their newest hero, with his mysterious new monster gun and his promise to destroy 'half of Israel' if Israel dares to attack him." This picture corresponded well to my own conclusions during my visit to the region in May-June 1990.

15. Ashraf Ghurbal interview with author, Cairo, Egypt, June 1990.

16. Statement by official spokesman of the Islamic deputies in the Jordanian House of Representatives, *FBIS* [Foreign Broadcast Information Service] *Daily Report*, May 10, 1990 (FBIS-NES-90).

17. Reports in Kuwaiti newspapers, *FBIS Daily Reports*, June 25, 1990 (FBIS-NES-90-122).

18. Statement by Hosni Mubarak, *FBIS Daily Report*, June 5, 1990 (FBIS-NES-90-108).

19. This was the assessment of several congressional aides and Middle East experts meeting in Washington, DC, a few days before the Iraqi invasion of Kuwait.

20. In my report to the chairman of the House Subcommittee on Europe and the Middle East, I concluded that Saddam Hussein had emerged as the most popular Arab leader.

21. Statement by Yasser Arafat at May 1990 Arab summit, *FBIS Daily Report*, July 11, 1990 (FBIS-NES-90).

22. Author's interview with Syrian and Egyptian officials, June 1990.

23. Yasser Arafat, interview with author, Baghdad, Iraq, June 1990.

24. Ariel Sharon was an Israeli army general who later became Prime Minister of Israel until a stroke incapacitated him. He was best remembered in the Arab world for his role as Israel's Defense Minister who led the Israeli invasion of Lebanon in 1982 against the forces of the Palestine Liberation Organization, and his role in the massacres of Palestinian civilians in two refugee camps. An Israeli commission found him indirectly responsible for the massacres and prohibited him from ever serving again as Defense Minister. The fear in the Arab world was that his real plan was to turn the Hashemite Kingdom of Jordan into a Palestinian state as a way of justifying maintaining control of the West Banks, which Israel occupied in 1967, and where (together with Gaza) Palestinians aspired to establish a state.

25. Statement by Yasser Arafat, *FBIS Daily Report*, May 29, 1990 (FBIS-NES-90).

26. Interviews with author, Amman, Jordan, June 1990.

27. Statement by King Hussein, *FBIS Daily Report*, May 30, 1990 (FBIS-NES-90).

28. Yasser Arafat and King Hussein were often opponents in Arab politics— including in the bloody confrontations between the King's forces and Palestinian groups in Jordan when the Jordanian army forced the PLO and other Palestinian groups to leave Jordanian territory. In following decades, there was always competition between the two on who represented the Palestinian people, even after the PLO was recognized by the Arab League in 1974 as the "sole, legitimate, representative of the Palestinian people."

29. Following an increase in food prices, a wave of Jordanian riots involving thousands swept through a number of Jordanian towns and resulted in the several deaths and dozens of injuries.

30. Kamal Abu Jaber, interview with author, Amman, Jordan, June 1990.

31. In explaining the riots, King Hussein seemed to blame Arab oil-producing states for failing to help Jordan, saying: "It is really the result of measures that had to be taken. We had to take some measures and obviously the people feel them. It is the result of the defaulting by certain Arab states in helping us," (Alan Cowell, "5 Are Killed in South Jordan as Rioting over Food Prices Spreads," *New York Times*, April 20, 1989, http://www.nytimes. com/1989/04/20/world/5-are-killed-in-south-jordan-as-rioting-over-foo d-prices-spreads.html).

32. This view was expressed by Yasser Arafat during our interview on June 5, 1990, as well as by several Jordanian analysts.

33. *Al-Ba'th*, Syrian Daily Newspaper (Arabic), 1990.

34. Interview with author, Damascus, Syria, May 30, 1990.

35. Usama Al-Baz, interview with author, Cairo, Egypt, 1990.

36. Woods, Palkki, and Stout, *The Saddam Tapes*, pp. 112–113.

37. Ibid., p. 110.

38. Ibid.

39. Ibid.

40. In one early episode in 1978, Hussein describes Arafat in this way, "As the Syrian slaughtered hundreds of men and large masses of the innocent Palestinians, Arafat did not move a whisker and was not the least shaken. This shows people the treason of Yasser Arafat and [just] who are Arafat's people.... Although the Arafat camp has conspired in every issue with which it was involved, there is no way we would engage in a battle with them or anyone that would harm the cause of Palestine" (ibid.).

41. Ibid., p. 137.

42. Jon Krosnick and Shibley Telhami, "Public Attitudes and American Policy toward Israel" (unpublished, 1992).

43. This account is based on a survey of the daily reports from the Arab world as published by the Foreign Broadcast Information Service. It should be noted that these reports are by no means comprehensive, because they reflect

mostly official and local press accounts, which could not be entirely reliable given the strict information control campaigns during the Gulf crisis. Nonetheless, this survey is useful as a limited indicator in conjunction with the analytical and first-hand accounts.

44. Both Algeria and Tunisia in North Africa were witnessing a rise in the power in Islamic parties that were challenging secular regimes backed by military establishments. These gains were in part a function of external pressure and local expectations following the end of the Cold War, where the United States and regional elites were pushing for democratization in the region. In fact the Islamists were poised for power in 1992 when the Algerian military moved to reverse the electoral process. In Tunisia, where there were no significant political openings, the regime used the Gulf crisis to ruthlessly crush the Islamist opposition.

45. In Egypt, many "Islamic" books, apparently funded by Gulf States, were published. Many of them found Iraq guilty on religious grounds and defended Egypt and Saudi Arabia: Muhammad Sayyid Tantawi (Egypt's Mufti), *Al-Hukm al-Shar'if i Ahdath al-Khalij* (Cairo: Dar al Ifta' al—Masriyya, 1990); Manna' Al-Qattan, *Harb al-Khalij fi Mizan al-Fiqh al Islami* (Cairo: al-Zahra' lil-'loom, 1991); Ahmad Omar Hashim (Deputy President of al-Azhar University), *Mihnata l-Khalij Wamawqif Misr Wassa'oodiyya Walbilad al-Islamiyya* (Cairo: Maktabat al-Turath al-Islami, 1991); Abd al-Halim 'uweis, *Ightiyala l-Kuweit* (Cairo: Dar al-Sahwa, 1991); and a collection of poems by Muhammada al-Tuhami, *Dima'al-"urooba'la Judrana l-Kuweit* (Cairo: Matabi'a l-ufset, 1991). Still, there were indications that public sentiment among the Islamic leaders was not unanimous. In the introduction to one of the books finding Iraq guilty on religious ground, the introduction (by Ahmad Ra'if) presents the author as "one of the few who did not hesitate to condemn the Iraqi invasion of Kuwait, speaking frankly and forcefully even though this hurt many of his friends and acquaintances who took a different stand" (Muhammad Salim al 'awwa, *Al-'abath bil-Islam fi Azamat al-Khalij* (Cairo: Al-Zahra' lil-I'lam al 'arabi, 1990), 9).

46. In my original 1993 article in *Political Science Quarterly*, I ended with the following conclusion: "If the Arab coalition falls apart and the Arab-Israeli peace process fails, the Arab public is likely to be mobilized again. And disagreements over the Gulf War (hidden feelings of guilt and resentment) are likely to surface. It is a mistake to conclude that the worse repercussions of the Gulf War have already come to pass."

47. For poll results, please visit http://www.sadat.umd.edu.

48. For a 1998 commentary on the cumulative impact of war and sanctions on Arab public opinion, see: http://sadat.umd.edu/pub/oped/Pax%20 Americana%20in%20the%20Middle%20East.htm.

INDEX

Printed and bound by CPI Group (UK) Ltd, Croydon, CR0 4YY